Bathe Seven Times

A Contemplative Look at the Seven Capital Sins

Mother Nadine

Published by Intercessors of the Lamb.

Additional copies may be obtained through our web page
or by contacting us:

Intercessors of the Lamb
4014 North Post Road
Omaha, NE 68112

Phone (402) 455-5262
Fax (402) 455-1323
E-mail: bellwether@novia.net
Web page: www.bellwetheromaha.org

ISBN 0-9664956-3-2

Published in the United States.

Table of Contents

Introduction

Scripture says Jesus set Mary Magdalene free "from seven demons" (Mk 16:9). He freed her from all of them. This is what we want to happen to us as well. We want to be freed from the roots of each of the Capital Sins. In 2 Kings there's a beautiful story of the leper Naaman, the army commander of the king of Aram. The prophet said, "Wash seven times in the Jordan" (2Kgs 5:10). Naaman didn't want to do what the prophet had said, but his servant begged him to do it, so he did. He bathed seven times in the Jordan and was totally reborn. His flesh became like a newborn child. This is what we want to do: we want to bathe seven times in the Living Water. We want to bathe seven times in these waters that will take us fully into the Promised Land, fully into the intimacy of God.

Somehow each of us has heard God calling us by name. God called Moses by name, "Moses, Moses." He called him twice. Maybe Moses didn't hear Him the first time, and maybe we don't hear God call us the first time either, but God doesn't mind repeating Himself. He has called each of us personally by name. Moses' response was, "Here I am" (Ex 3:4). Isn't that beautiful? That's our response, too: "Here I am."

Each of us has received a call. When we talk about a call, we're talking about a mission as well. We have a mission. Moses was called to be a prayer warrior and a tremendous intercessor, but first and foremost, he was called as a prophet to listen to God and dialogue with Him. This is where he received his instructions.

As we study the Capital Sins, we will constantly be going back to our relationship with God because without this relationship, we haven't any life, we haven't any power, we haven't anything because Jesus is everything. We are called to the summit of love—we are called to transforming union. We are called to be totally one with Jesus Christ, especially Jesus Christ Crucified who is the summit of agape love, because Jesus is *the* Prayer Warrior. Jesus is *the* Intercessor. Jesus is *the* Mediator. Jesus is the Beloved Son, the One whom the Father listens to. So when Jesus prays in us and through us and with us, we know we have

1

the Father's ear. So this mission that we have is one like Moses' mission, but first and foremost it is a call to relationship.

When God spoke of the mission to Moses, He said, "I will send you to Pharaoh to lead My people, the Israelites, out of Egypt" (Ex 3:10). "I will send you" really catches my attention. What is different now is that He wants to send us. We have had the armor on, or at least parts of it on, for so long. When we are severely attacked, we may begin to wonder, "What happened to the helmet? What happened to the shield? What happened to me?" But hopefully, we have the armor on. God is saying, "I will send *you.*" He's talking about sending us forth now as prayer warriors right into the enemy's camp to lead His people out of Egypt, out of paganism, out of the desert, and out of all the places where they are confined right now.

The beautiful words God gave to Moses on Mount Sinai, He gives to us, too. He promised Moses, "I will be with you" (Ex 3:12). It is key for a prayer warrior to understand, "I will be with you." We need to believe it. If we don't believe that God is with us, then we're going to go down fast because when the thick of the battle comes and the clouds get dark Satan will know right away that we're not really sure. "Lord, where are You?" We don't have to say that if we believe His promise to us that He is always with us. "You're not going to go into battle alone" is what He is telling us, "because the battle belongs to Me. It's My battle, but I need to fight it through, with, and in you now. I will be with you." And our response is "Lord, I believe You. I truly believe in You. I know You wouldn't call me to this kind of ministry, to this mission, if You weren't true to Your promise that You will be with me always, always, whether the sun is shining or not."

He is forming us deeply as prayer warriors. He wants to heal us so that when we come against the enemy, the doors within our own houses where the enemy could enter will be closed so we won't get hurt or knocked down. Many times people take a beating in this kind of ministry, and we wonder, "Lord, what's happening here? There must be some open doors." There are open doors within all of us, so we're going to try to get those doors closed so we can all be fully armed, with our houses fully locked up except for the presence of the Lord. He wants us to be prepared and well trained so we can go forth with the Sword, with Jesus Himself, and not only fight the battle but win.

St. Paul tells us that God chose us from the very beginning of the world to be holy and blameless in His sight (see Eph 1:4). In other words, Paul is telling us that to be a saint is simply to be full of God's love. Sometimes we are so full of our own self-love, self-interest, and self-concern, but we are called to be saints. We may wonder what is God's will. I hear people asking us this very often. The answer is very simple. Paul tells us that God's will is our sanctification. It is to be holy. It is to become a saint. This is all throughout the Bible. The Father Himself tells us, "You shall be holy because I am holy" (Lv 11:45). It's so simple, isn't it? He wants us to be holy because He wants us to be like Himself. Everything He has He wants to give us. He has given us everything in the tremendous gift of Jesus, so we need to take a closer look at the reasons why we are not yet as holy as God wants us to be.

It's extremely important that we know who we are because if we don't know, Satan will try to tell us who we are. We have all heard some of those accusations. They can make us very unsteady and wobbly if we really don't know who we are. Many times we have come up against Satan himself in spiritual warfare ministry, and one of the main things he will always say is, "Who do you think you are?" Have you ever heard that? Now it would be terrible if we said, "Oh, I don't know who I really am." We do know who we are.

One of Satan's titles in Scripture is Lucifer, which means "angel of light" (2Cor 11:14). Obviously it means deceiver; this is how cunning he is. He will deceive us with light, not with things that look evil, dark, or really bad, but with light. This is a tremendous deception. This is one reason why the experience at Mount Tabor, to be bathed and clothed and transfigured in light as Jesus was, is so important for us.

Jesus tells us very clearly, "Be on guard and pray that you may not undergo the test" (Mt 26:41). I think this is extremely important for prayer warriors to know: watch and pray that we enter not into temptation. This watchfulness and prayerfulness actually become weapons for us because temptation is the doorway into sin. We don't usually step right into sin. First we step into the doorway, into temptation. This is where the struggle takes place. This is where a choice is made. Jesus taught us to pray to the Father, "Subject us not to the trial but deliver us from the evil one" (Mt 6:13). "Don't even let us get close, Father.

Protect us." If we make the wrong choice, then we pass through that doorway of temptation into sin itself, which is usually stepping into Satan's kingdom. When we give into temptation and are led into sin, it weakens our posture and our ability to stand firm. It weakens our ability to hold fast, to hold our ground, and because we are on shaky territory, we can easily fall or move into full sin.

So one of Satan's main strategies is that he lies, as Jesus has told us. He distorts God's word. He distorts God's truth. He is the father of lies (see Jn 8:44) and attempts to invalidate God's word. This is what he did when he tempted Eve. He said, "Did God really tell you not to eat from any of the trees in the garden?" (Gn 3:1) He tried to invalidate what God had said. Eve dialogued with him, which is one of the main principles of a prayer warrior: *never dialogue with Satan*. But Eve did. She took a step a little too close and gave Satan the information that he was looking for. He didn't know all that God had said to Eve in that pure light. He didn't know, but she told him. "Oh no," she said, "God didn't say that. God said this." Then Satan invalidated God's word by saying, "Oh that's because God doesn't want you to be like Himself" (see Gn 3:1-6), and so Eve believed the lie.

The truth is that God *does* want us to be like Him; that's why He sent Jesus. God wants us to have His mind, His heart, His will, His preference, and His plan. He wants to share His life fully and totally with us, but He doesn't want us to be God. Sin comes in when we try to be God. Sin comes in when we forget that He is the Creator, and we are the creatures. Sin comes in when we forget He is our Father, and we are His children, His little ones.

Jesus was without sin, and so the enemy had no hold on Him, none whatsoever. The enemy only operates in the territory of sin. This is what he lives and breathes. He tries to entice us to be where he is, but God is calling us to walk in holiness. Scripture says, "In Him there is no darkness" (1Jn 1:5). Isn't that beautiful? He was filled perfectly, totally, fully with light. One time the Lord showed me that when Jesus was led into the desert by the Holy Spirit, the Holy Spirit led Him right into Satan's camp. But it's interesting that face-to-face with enemy number one, Satan couldn't touch Jesus. He tried to tempt Him, but it didn't work because Jesus was clothed in light. He had on the armor of light because He is light. The Holy Spirit is going to be leading us right into Satan's camp, also. The more we can be filled with God's

4

light and truth, the more the darkness within us and others will be dispelled. Satan won't be able to get hooked into us.

So many times when we are praying with people and interceding for people, we see that there are places within them that are still in darkness. Satan is there in his insidious little ways with his cohorts tempting, controlling, or keeping people in bondage, or he is going in and out of the house in the dark areas ministering to people. Studying and pondering the Capital Sins will bring God's light into every area of our entire being.

First St. Paul said, "Let us cast off deeds of darkness" (Rom 13:12), and then he said, "Put on the armor of light" (Rom 13:12). Once we cast out deeds of darkness and God's light comes into us, Satan doesn't have a platform within us anymore. Bringing God's light is the easiest way to do deliverance ministry. Satan and his cohorts will flee. They hate the light. They're like bats. Bats don't do well in light, but they are very powerful in the dark. So the light is our number one weapon to dispel the darkness and uproot Satan.

Sin will always be an infraction of God's love in some way. It will always bear the bad fruit of coming against God's love: it will make us somehow love God less, love ourselves less and love others less. It will always strike against love. God really wants us to know our enemy in all the areas in which he lurks and hides. Satan loves concealment; he doesn't want to be evicted. The evil spirits like to live within people; they don't like to live outside of us. The reason must be because living within us is the greatest way they can strike at Jesus. The evil spirits may choose to live within us, but God also chooses to dwell within us if we allow Him. The light will reveal who they are and where they are.

Our community went through a study of the Capital Sins. We called it "Sin Formation," but when we called it this, people looked so shocked that we thought we'd better find another name! The Lord indicated that He wanted sin rooted out of us now so we could be totally free from Satan's camp. He wanted us to be totally free to live and move and have our being available to counteract Satan. He didn't want us to put band-aids on our sins anymore but He wanted to start rooting sin out. He wants us to be a garden enclosed so that we can re-enter into the Promised Land within.

We found that there were secondary roots of each of the sins, but the deeper root of all of them was fear. This is when I began to realize that this must be why Jesus talked so much in the Gospels about fear. "Fear not. Fear not, little flock. Do not fear. Fear is useless." He was giving us the main weapon, His love, to come against fear. "Perfect love casts out all fear" (1Jn 4:18), and of course only God's love is perfect love. So God is the Deliverer and with His love He will uproot the fear within us. This fear is based upon Satan's lies, whereas God's love is based upon truth. So whenever we are with Jesus and adhered to Him, we are on a firm foundation because Jesus is the Rock. Jesus is Truth. Nothing can shake a house (and each of us individually is God's house) that is built on rock, but we have to be careful if we're building our house on the lie, on fear, because then we are on shifting sand.

The enemy, called the dragon, is described as having seven heads (Rv 12:3). One way of looking at this is to equate the seven heads with the Seven Capital Sins. "The dragon became angry at the woman and went off to wage war against the rest of her offspring, on those who keep God's commandments and give witness to Jesus" (Rv 12:17). Now the woman's offspring would be us. Hopefully we're trying to keep God's commandments, hopefully we're trying to witness to Jesus, and so the dragon is angry and is going off to make war upon us. Scripture says that he took up his position on the sand of the seashore (see Rv 12:18). When I first read this the Lord let me understand that Satan doesn't have a good foothold at all. He's building on a sandy shore, and sand can move. We wouldn't ever want to build on sand. Jesus has been very clear that we are to build our house upon the Rock.

Jesus' light is key. When a room is totally dark, and we flip on the light switch, the darkness is gone instantly. It's gone instantly, not gradually. This is what God's light will do to our darkness. We want to invite Him into each of these areas of sin, into these areas of darkness within us, and ask Him to bring His light. When He brings His light, He comes in truth, and His truth will set us free.

Format

These chapters have been put into two-part categories. First, we will study the capital sin and how it shows up and manifests itself in our everyday lives and in our spiritual lives. The second part will focus on the remedies to help us fight this sin. We will study the gift of the Holy Spirit that has already been given to us at Confirmation that will be the power to come against this sin. Then we will focus on one of the seven words of Jesus on the Cross because Calvary is the actual weapon against sin. The event that we always celebrate is Calvary. Calvary is where sin was put to death. This is where we have to put it to death with that Sword of the Spirit, Jesus. Then we will focus on the virtues that are needed to produce the fruit to help counteract the fruit of the sin. We will end each section with an Examination of Conscience to help us recognize and become more aware of sin in our lives.

Chapter 1

Anger

One time the Lord gave me an image of little black-gray clouds, kind of wispy and flimsy. I could still see the moon on the other side of the clouds but not in its full brilliance and light because of the clouds passing in front of it. The Lord let me understand this is exactly what sin does to our souls. In many ways our souls are like the moon, reflecting God's light, reflecting the sun/Son and the beauty, but even the slightest shade of sin can mar that light. Sin can mar and affect how much our souls are going to reflect Him and how much of His light is going to shine through each one of us. When we see sin in this light, we don't want any shade of sin on our souls at all. We don't want anything to mar that beauty of the fullness of the moon reflecting the fullness of God's love, light, and grace.

All our emotions are God-given gifts. We are made in His image and likeness (see Gn 1:27). God has beautiful feelings, and He has shared them with us. No emotion of itself is a sin. We cannot directly control the arising of an emotion in our hearts. It just happens. It's a feeling. But we can choose the way we are going to use that emotion. We can choose what we are going to do with it. Our will can command any emotion to rise, to flourish, or to cease. If the commands that we give to this emotion are weak, they will not be obeyed because we will allow our emotions to be stronger than our will.

We can't control our first impulse or emotion that arises, but our will can command that emotion to rise or to cease. We have control over our emotions if we choose to use our will. So our choice of what we do with our emotion can make it virtuous, or it can make it a vice. When we are not using the gift of our emotions for God's greater honor and glory, then Satan will come and use them for his. Our consent or lack of consent is what is going to make our emotions either sinful or virtuous. It can go either way. We need to exercise our will.

The first time I became aware of not being able to control that first thought or emotion was a simple teaching the Lord gave me in the cloister novitiate. The sisters were out walking at noon recreation with our novice mistress. We were walking under the trees in the orchard, and a bird dropping dropped on her black veil. Well, no one could control that. It was something that just happened, but how we respond to what happens is something we can control. This novice mistress controlled her emotions beautifully and used it to teach us right then. We can respond to situations in our lives in anger and get terribly upset (you don't get something like that out overnight in one of these black veils, and it was right on top!), but she used her feelings beautifully, in a virtuous way, as a teaching for her little pupils who were out walking with her. This helped me understand that we can't control our first emotion anymore than we can control our first thought, but we *can* control how we respond. That's our choice.

Anger arising from zeal is virtuous, but anger arising from passion is sinful. We see God's anger arises from His zeal, His tremendous love for souls, for goodness, for life, for what is right, and for whatever glorifies the Father. This is virtuous anger. So getting angry righteously at the right things is not a sin (getting angry at the wrong things is a sin). We see this beautifully in the way God manifests His anger. Jesus got very angry more than once. One of the classic times is when He was angry with the moneychangers in the temple. Well, He's in our temple, and when He sees us shortchanging God, He can get upset with us, too. This is a justified anger. It's a controlled anger. It's God's anger. One way to tell if our anger is being led by the Spirit, we can ask ourselves, "Am I getting angry at things I should be getting angry at? Is my anger controlled?" Because if our anger is Spirit-led, it will be Spirit-controlled as well. As long as our anger is controlled by God, it can serve a very fruitful purpose.

One time I experienced God's anger when I was praying a Rosary with the community a few years ago. I started to feel tremendous anger within. It frightened me because I had never experienced anger at this level. I asked the Lord, "What is this? What's going on?" We happened to be praying a Rosary for the Supreme Court of the United States, and God was very angry, particularly about the abortion issue. He was even letting us know how to pray because of His anger. There is a power in God's anger, and when we're sharing in that anger, there is a power in our prayer. Many times God directs us when we are in spiritual warfare by His own feelings. He has all of these emotions; this is how we got them. He is sharing them with us.

Not too long ago someone asked me, "How can God get angry because anger can lead to hate? How can this happen because God is love?" This is a good question. Philosophically I can't answer that, but what I can answer is that God is love. Because God loves, He can hate anything that's going to destroy, harm, lessen, or decrease that love. It is out of love that we can also become angry, which can lead to hate.

God taught me this while in the cloister. We had a beautiful cat named Mademoiselle who was given to my care. We couldn't let the cat roam the cloister freely because our superior had received a German Shepherd, Duke, from some people who wanted us to keep it for them. They didn't want to put the dog to sleep. We couldn't let this cat roam the cloister freely from one room to another because if the dog caught her, we knew he would kill her. So we had to carry the cat or keep her cat confined.

So at recreation times, the sisters were very careful to make sure that Duke was inside so Mademoiselle had a chance to go out. And when Mademoiselle was in, Duke was out. One time we were out and I was carrying her in my arms. I asked, "Is Duke in?" They said, "Yes, we haven't seen him around, so he must be in." I put the cat down, and all of a sudden, Duke appeared over the horizon. He saw all of us. He saw Mademoiselle wandering off. She hadn't seen him yet. We knew he could get to her before we could, and the sisters became paralyzed. It was a moment of silence.

Then Duke went into action. If you've ever seen a German Shepherd go into action, you know what I mean. He was going lickety-split for her. The sisters, paralyzed with fear, started screaming at the top of their lungs. If you can imagine, fifty-some sisters screaming! And the more they screamed, the more they frightened the cat, still unaware that the dog was after her. So Mademoiselle stopped for a moment, and when she stopped, that's all Duke needed to pounce. In the meantime, I took off running after the dog. As he flew through the air to pounce at her throat, I flew through the air to grab his tail.

But the emotion I experienced at that moment, for the first time in my life, was hate. I hated what he was going to do because I loved that cat. When I flew through the air and yanked his tail

11

with both hands as hard as I could, he was so surprised that he lessened his jaws from her throat for just a moment. Mademoiselle had gotten the picture by now and was way up a tree.

I was really shaken over this because I thought, "Oh Lord, that's hate." I had never experienced the emotion of hate before. It's a strong emotion, and I've experienced it several times since in deliverance ministry. Hate takes away all fear because when you love someone or something so much you'll do anything to save that person or thing. We have a vow of zeal for the salvation of souls. Hatred for sin and what Satan is doing can actually become so powerful within us that we won't be afraid. This is more the good part of anger and hatred; it's God's holy anger. However, we must go to any measure necessary to stop anger that is going to manifest itself in a way that would be harmful to someone or something.

Recently I was asked, "Can we hate a person's philosophy and ideas but not hate the person?" God always separates the sin from the sinner, and we certainly can, too. There are times when we certainly should feel angry about what is going on in our world. It should anger us enough that we want the injustice stopped. We hate what is happening, but we don't hate the person. We always have to distinguish between the two.

It's interesting that God can hate. There always needs to be discernment in the emotions because God is love. God can hate anything that will try to destroy love, and so there are things that we hate. We should hate the things that try to destroy God's love, particularly God's love in people. From the beginning, prayer warriors need to learn to separate the person from their actions. We can hate what the actions are but never hate the person. We don't want to destroy what God has made. We always want to pray that love will come into that person or situation. If we start hating people and not what they do, and if we can't separate the sin from the sinner, then we have gone into Satan's camp right away and lost that round of the battle.

The first time I experienced this was in the cloister with a superior who had two sets of rules: the rule that all of us followed, the written rule approved by the Church, and the unwritten rule for her own little group. Because I was her assistant, I saw this dynamic up very close, and it really bothered me. Anger was growing very deeply within me at this double standard, this hypocrisy that I was watching every day. I saw a lot of things up close, but because I was her assistant and loyal to her, I couldn't really talk about it. I couldn't help the other sisters the way they needed to be helped even though I felt they were being victimized. I was caught in the middle, as intercessors often are.

The superior was very intuitive, as most contemplatives are, and she began to sense that I was not approving of what she was doing even though I wasn't saying anything. One evening I was in my room, and she knocked at my door and gave me a little present to make everything all right. I thanked her, closed the door, and all of a sudden, the emotion was just too much for me. I blurted out to the Lord, "I hate her." I was shocked at myself! I had never hated anybody. I couldn't believe I said what I said, but I did. I even said it out loud, so obviously there was a lot of anger that had been building up over weeks and weeks that had not been handled.

I had said this to the Lord with such intense emotion that it frightened me enough that I went to the Lord quickly. I thought, "I had better get to the Lord. This is not good. I'm not at a good place here at all. I need to find out what's going on." Had I taken this to the Lord earlier, I probably wouldn't have gotten such an intense response that was now coming out as hate. So immediately I went to the chapel, and He gave me an image of my mother giving me a very good spanking when I was four years old. As a little four-year-old, I was crying out, "I hate you. I hate you because you're touching your own flesh and blood this way." Evidently I thought that was wrong. Well, you don't get very far when you're screaming at your parent anyway.

I said to the Lord, "What was I doing to get a spanking like that in the first place?" He said (when I say, "He said," I mean that He illumines my mind with truth), "Well, you were running away all the time. You were in rebellion. You were disobedient. You deserved it." All that emotion was still deep within me, and the Lord showed me what the dynamic was. "You didn't hate your mother, but you felt she was abusing her authority as parent. You don't hate your superior, but you feel she, too, is abusing her authority." Both situations were the same: two women whom I really loved, but I felt they were both abusing their authority.

It wasn't my mother that I hated, and it wasn't my superior that I hated. It was the abuse of authority that I hated. This light, this truth brought me instant peace. Then I could pray that my superior would get lights to use her authority correctly. I began to

13

see what God meant—we can love somebody but still hate what he or she is doing. As these emotions were coming up, the Lord was showing me how to separate what people do from who people are. This is very important to do when we're dealing with our emotions, particularly anger, because there are a lot of things we don't like, and we have to be careful to separate that from the person. We don't criticize that person, but we take the person or situation to the Lord for that light on how to pray. This is what prayer warriors do. Our greatest power is in prayer.

This is one reason why journaling is so important. Obviously, I was not taking my initial anger at my superior to the journal. I was just keeping it in and wasn't taking it anywhere because I felt it would be disloyal to her as her assistant. Had I taken it to the journal, it might not have built up the way it did, but the Lord used it to teach me a very important lesson.

I had another experience around this time to do with anger and learning to take it to the Lord. I had asked one of the sisters in the cloister if she would help me in the altar bread room after supper. I wanted to join the sisters, who were going to the other side of the convent, to jump around on the trampoline and have fun in the gym. As cloistered nuns we didn't get to do this very often. I was in charge of the altar bread room and thought that if I could just get a little help then I could join the sisters, too.

So when I asked her if she would help me for a few minutes after supper, she said no. I did a lot of favors for the sisters so it never dawned on me that any sister would say no. It never even entered my mind. I said, "No?" She said, "Yes, I'm going over to the gym. No." I really could feel things being stirred up within me. I thought, "Lord, I never refuse a sister anything. How could a sister refuse another sister?" I was mumbling and fuming. After supper that night, I went to the altar bread room to do what I had to do and was there for about two minutes when another sister came along the corridor on her way to the gym. She stopped and said, "Do you need any help?" I said, "Oh yes, I could use some help." She helped me and five minutes later we both were free.

But I didn't go to the gym that night. I went up and spent some time with the Lord because this emotion of anger was stirred up. I thought, "Lord, I don't want Satan to get a hold of me. Help me. I don't like this kind of anger. Show me what's happening here." So I took it to Him and asked Him for His light. I asked, "Did You hear the conversation?" "Yes." "You heard her answer?"

14

"Yes." "Lord, tell me what You think. What did You hear?" He let me understand that she was a very high-strung, nervous sister. I said, "Yes, she is." He said, "And you know that being in the gym would really help her release so much of her tension." "Oh yes, I can see that now. It would be very good for her." He said, "And that would help her become a better community sister, wouldn't it?" "Well, yes it would." "Well," He said, "I sent you some help, didn't I, in the altar bread room?" "Oh yes, You did." He said, "Well, then what's your problem?" It was gone! It was gone. There is a lot of wisdom in not letting the sun go down on our anger. We have to get it out. If we keep it in, it will come out in other ways. Rather we should take it to the Lord where His light and truth can come and dispel it.

We are talking specifically about the capital sin of anger. The Church and many of the saints teach us that anger itself isn't the worst sin, but anger is a capital sin because it opens the door and leads to other sins. It's the gate. Sometimes when we give into our anger, Satan takes over, and we're out of control. Then we are usually in the enemy's camp. It opens the door to other sins and manifestations of anger, with hate being the very worst of all the manifestations of anger. The last stage of anger is hate, and if we stay there, it can become diabolical. It is the opposite of love, and Satan usually is controlling us then.

There are four levels of anger. The first is only the emotion of anger. It might be that someone has a bad temper. They're just hot- or quick-tempered. It could be their nationality or disposition. They flare up easily, but it is only the emotion. The second level is anger that is regulated by reason. This is when our will is involved. This is a deeper level of anger because our will is involved now—which way are we going to go with the anger? The third level of anger oversteps the bounds of right reason, and we can get out of control here. This is what St. Thomas Aquinas calls the capital sin of anger. It's more serious. It's over-stepping the bounds of right reason. The fourth level of anger is when our emotion of anger turns to hatred of God and/or neighbor.

What Anger Looks Like in Me

Once I took a course at Creighton University on the emotions. When we got on the subject of anger, we were given another vocabulary for anger. I found it very helpful because I came from a family where anger was never expressed. I had very gentle, loving parents and a very happy home life. To my understanding, anger was like in the movies when someone was shouting and screaming and ranting and raving. I never saw that in my home, so I was not able to get in touch with my own anger. I thought, "I don't do that. How do I know if I'm angry or not?" I couldn't identify it.

Anger has many faces, and it is going to look a little bit different in each one of us. So we have to "put our head in our heart" and take a look, asking the Holy Spirit to flash His flashlight there to show us how anger manifests itself in us. We need to know how anger manifests itself within myself personally.

We have quite a vocabulary for anger, and we each need to find the words that we use to help us identify anger in our lives. If someone says, "I'm outraged" or "I feel used," we know they are pretty angry. "I'm repulsed." "I'm furious." "I'm resentful." "I'm frustrated, annoyed, irritated, perturbed, provoked, upset, disappointed, exasperated, uptight, peeved." Even, "I'm disappointed" can be a very subtle way of really saying, "I'm angry at you."

Usually an unhappy person has some anger deep within. If there's a loss of peace, we can go right into anger if we're not careful. We will see anger as discord in families, communities, or within ourselves. Anger can also express itself in sadness, bitterness, sarcasm, stubbornness, quarrels, unforgiveness, and retaliation. Anger expresses itself in always taking the opposite side, not agreeing on anything, holding grudges, nit-picking, saying abusive words and insulting comments, nursing injuries, and seeking revenge (a more serious expression of anger).

We see retaliation a lot with the enemy, but humanly we can retaliate, too. The Lord reminded me of a time when I retaliated against my brother when I was seven years old. We had identical twin cats, Amos and Andy. My brother, who was ten, cut the whiskers off my cat. Those whiskers are really important to a cat to help it navigate in the dark, so my cat went around bumping into everything. I thought, "What do I do? How can I get even?" I wasn't going to go up and hit my brother. He was much bigger than I was and he would just hit me back. We really were good friends, except now I was pretty unhappy with him. I couldn't believe he had done this to my cat. I knew his favorite hobby was making model airplanes. He would work for hours in his room gluing those things together. So I took one of his little model airplanes and put it under my grandmother's rocking chair. After dinner that night when my grandmother went in to sit down in the rocking chair, she rocked on that little airplane and smashed it to smithereens. I was perfectly innocent. He couldn't blame me; it was my grandmother who did it. So now that I'm all grown up, and the Lord took me back to that memory and said, "You were angry. You didn't know any other way to get back. That's retaliation."

Impatience will be a sign that we are falling into anger. It might not be full-blown anger, but when we start getting impatient we're on our way. We see this in very serious ways, which has even led to road rage. Anger will hinder our right use of reason, and then it will go into the capital sin and will violate God's love. Anger has a negative effect on others, and it will always lead to uncharitableness.

Angry thoughts lead to angry conduct. We see this full-blown with Jesus' crucifixion. It began with a lot of thoughts that the scribes and Pharisees started having, escalated into speech, and then into action on their part. Anger leads to a spirit of contradiction. It leads to rudeness. Sometimes anger might be manifested in just being withdrawn. It can lead to lying, concealment, and faultfinding.

I had a superior who used to say, "I can't hear a word you're saying because your actions are shouting." This can happen. Sometimes we might not say anything, but our actions say it. We might know someone else is angry not by what they're saying but by their actions or by what they're not saying. We need to know which adjectives fit us. How does anger express itself within me? What does it look like? We want to give a face to our sins because Satan knows us so well, and he goes about like a roaring lion seeking someone to devour. We need to know what's going on within us. If we don't, we can build a house of anger within ourselves by not dealing with these different expressions of anger. If we do that, evil spirits can come and live or "minister" to us like we are their playthings.

In My Spiritual Life

Sometimes people are afraid to tell us or to tell anyone who they are angry or upset with God. But many times we are angry with God. Job was very upset with God. Many of the saints would get upset with God. But God sees us as little children, and little children can get their anger out to a parent, can't they? The parent isn't going to love them any less because they're angry with them. God doesn't love us any less. He can handle our anger.

But He knows that *we* can't handle our anger at Him. We have to get it out. So if we are upset with God about different things, the first thing we do - we tell Him about it. We journal it out. We write it out. "This is what I don't like. This is what I hate. This is what I wish You would have done that You didn't do. I can't understand why You allowed this. Why did You give me these parents? Why weren't You there when I needed you as a little child? Why was I adopted? Why was I rejected? Where were You when I had no one and You were not there for me? Where were You?" Sometimes we might be upset with something the Church is doing or something it isn't doing, or something a priest has done or didn't do, or something a nun did or didn't do. There are many ways of being upset with God and His representatives.

Whatever it is, we get it out because as long as we're upset or angry with God, we're not going to hear a word He is saying to us. These are authentic questions that we need to ask God in our journaling; we need to hear from God. Then God's grace will start to flow. Hearing from God will be the healing itself. But we have a tendency not to talk about our anger, and so we turn our back on God. We give Him the silent treatment because we're angry with Him, and the pain continues. The root can grow and the wound can fester. Sometimes people are afraid to let God know that they're angry with Him, but no one knows better than God Himself does that we're upset with Him! We need to get our emotions out, and then God will start to minister to us in this area. He may show us why He made a certain decision or why He didn't do something. He may show us that He was there all the time, but we didn't know it. He will let us know.

Spiritual Warfare

There are many evil spirits that manifest themselves in this capital sin of anger. There is a high-powered controlling spirit of anger itself. There are spirits of hate, rage, blasphemy, murder, violence, turbulence, conflict, death, hostility, destruction, and division. Division will always be one of the fruits of anger as it severs our relationships with God and others. We encounter a spirit of mockery quite frequently; it is a repressed spirit of anger. It will come out in giddiness or laughter that isn't appropriate at the time.

Satan constantly uses a spirit of retaliation with people who pray, particularly prayer warriors. In Revelation 12:17 we read that Satan was angry at the woman (angry at the Church, angry at all of us), and so he was going off to wage war on her offspring (us). He is going to retaliate. A spirit of retaliation is a spirit that is very angry and it's going to strike back because somehow we have advanced into Satan's kingdom and Satan is upset. He will use another spirit to retaliate.

For example, if we've been in prayer ministry and have won some kind of victory, we might begin to feel very, very fatigued. The spirit of retaliation may be striking back at us, using a spirit of fatigue because with a fatigued spirit, it's going to be very difficult to pray. We are going to fall asleep every time we pray. This is a very effective way to stop a prayer warrior. Many times the spirit of retaliation will attack a prayer warrior using a spirit of anger or depression. When one spirit uses another spirit, it is important to remember to bind all the spirits. Since the spirit of retaliation is so hidden, it is easy to miss. So we need to go after both spirits. So we bind the spirit of retaliation and the spirit it is working through.

We find that Satan retaliates constantly when we are in prayer ministry. As we become more sensitive to the Holy Spirit, He will constantly alert us to what evil spirits are speaking to us through others or when they are even speaking to us personally. There is a coldness there, and we know that this isn't the Lord.

Remedies

Gift of the Holy Spirit: Piety

Even though we received all the gifts of the Holy Spirit at Confirmation, they can lie dormant within us if we are not using them. We need to constantly activate these gifts through prayer. The gift of the Holy Spirit of Piety will counteract anger. It has been given to us as a weapon to help us cast out anger. It is a tremendous gift of great love of the Father and His children. This gift lets us really know the Father, love the Father, and to be able to call Him "Abba." It is when we are so in love with the Father, so connected with Him, that we desire to always do whatever pleases Him and whatever He is asking of us.

The gift of Piety reaches out as that peacemaker to others at all times. It's a two-fold gift of love. The gift of Piety took Jesus to the Cross and kept Him there. At Calvary, the gift we see Jesus having more than any other is Piety. At Calvary we see His great love of the Father and His great love of souls, being the Peacemaker. Jesus knew His identity. He was not the Father—He was the Son. He was child. In this gift of Piety, we come to know our true identity as prayer warriors. We are children of the Lord. We are God's children.

This gift of Piety gives us the motive, the strength, and the direction to nail anger to the Cross. Why? It's not for myself—that wouldn't be enough motive. We would cling and hold onto our anger. But the gift of Piety helps us release it for the greater honor and glory of the Father and for the salvation of souls. Piety is a beautiful gift that we need to combat the capital sin of anger and to lay that sin to rest with Jesus on the Cross.

Generally children can forgive quite easily and very quickly. They don't hold grudges. We can call upon this gift of piety because we have already received it at Confirmation. We need to use it and let the Spirit use it within us so we can forgive quickly and easily.

Words from the Cross

Our number one weapon is the Cross. We are victim lambs, and the event we are celebrating is Calvary. The first word from the Cross, "Father, forgive them for they do not know what they are doing" (Lk 23:34) is our number one weapon against anger.

One of the reasons we have so much trouble forgiving is rooted in fear. Our anger is rooted in fear. If we can stay angry, it's safe. But if I let go my anger, the fear is "Am I going to be hurt again? Do I have to have another encounter again with this person? Who's going to step on my heart this time?" There is always a fear that will keep us from forgiving, and so the power of Calvary is extremely important in our lives because it's pure love power. It's the summit of all love. Only perfect love can drive out that fear. With Jesus, we can nail anger to the Cross. We can nail it. We can totally uproot it when we can say, "Father, forgive them for they do not know what they're doing." We can't pray that unless we forgive and let it go. In that forgiveness anger is put to death right then and there. We lay the ax to the root by taking our anger right to the Cross.

We need divine love power from on High to forgive. To forgive is not natural; it's supernatural. It's a divine gift. This is why they didn't have to forgive in the Old Testament. They didn't have to turn the other cheek. It was an eye for an eye and a tooth for a tooth. But Jesus comes along and says, "That's all different now. You have to forgive. You have to turn the other cheek." This was new to the Apostles, and Peter asks, "Lord, when my brother wrongs me, how often must I forgive him? Seven times?" "No," Jesus replied "not seven times; I say, seventy times seven times" (Mt 18:22). We are to forgive over and over and over again. This seemed impossible, but nothing is impossible to God because the power to love comes from God, and it's ours for the asking.

The first word Jesus said from the Cross has given us this power. He won this grace for us when He said, "Father, forgive them for they do not know what they're doing" (Lk 23:34). One time He told me, "I won this grace for you. I won it. All you have to do is ask Me now for the grace. It's yours for the asking. Now there is no justification in unforgiveness because you have the way open for the grace to forgive."

St. Paul understood this when he said, "If you forgive a man anything, so do I. Any forgiving I have done has been for your sakes and, before Christ, to prevent Satan—whose guile we know too well—from outwitting us" (2Cor 2:10-11). Paul knew that not to forgive left the door wide open for Satan, leaving a legal platform for Satan to come in and keep stirring up anger. Sometimes we can think of a million reasons not to forgive.

One time some very dear friends of mine said something that was quite negative and hurtful about me. Because they were friends, it really hurt. Strangers could have said the same thing, and it wouldn't have hurt so much. The deepest pains we experience usually come from the people we love. This comment was said to my spiritual director, and he shared it with me so I knew that they had really said it. He thought that I should go to their house to reconcile. I said, "I don't think I can do that, Father. I'm the victim here of their sin. They have said something very hurtful, and it's not even true. Don't you think they should come and apologize to me?" He was very wise, very holy. He said, "Why don't you just pray about it and see what the Lord shows you." When we don't have the grace, we don't have the grace. He knew I didn't have the grace and needed to get it from God.

So I asked the Lord, "What about this situation? Do You actually want me to apologize for this distancing and separation that's happened between us when it really wasn't my fault?" He gave me an image of Himself on the Cross and said, "No one apologized to Me." Well, I went! I high-tailed it over there so fast it wasn't funny because Jesus forgave and forgave and forgave and no one apologized to Him.

When I walked in their home, God had their hearts prepared, also. They didn't have the grace to step out first, but once I came they did have the grace. They interrupted me as I started to apologize for the distancing and anything that I had done that was causing this separation and division. They said, "No, we're the ones who need to apologize." It was kind of a double apology, and we have been friends ever since. This put the enemy to death right there.

In order to be healed of our anger, oftentimes we have to go through a dying process. We go through five basic stages in the healing process. The first stage is denial. We try to tell ourselves that we're not really angry. I believe this is the most difficult stage because we're not going to get healed if we are pretending something doesn't bother us. We go through the denial and then try to get out of it on our own. Thanks be to God, my spiritual director helped me a great deal to get out of this stage of denial by showing me the different ways that I was angry and denying it.

So the next stage that we will go into is anger itself because it has surfaced now. The memories have surfaced and anger is coming forth. Satan loves this anger, and he'll try to keep us angry. "That's right," Satan will say, "you were justified in saying what you said. Don't forgive. Stay angry."

After we get the anger out, we will go into the third stage as we begin bargaining with God. This is where journaling is so helpful. We tell God about the situation, how we are feeling, and then we hear from God. We usually will try to bargain because we want to justify how right we are, but it doesn't work. Jesus is Jewish and He can out-bargain us any day! So when we don't win at the bargaining, the fourth stage, which is depression, because there isn't any place else to go now. Hopefully we won't stay in this stage too long because the reality comes—"I'd better let it go." This is the fifth stage. It's in the letting go that we can really say, "Forgive me, Father. Give me the grace to forgive them." Then we come into peace and freedom.

The Cross entails a dying process for us, but this dying process is extremely important because it is the very power of intercession. It holds the victory over anger. Luke 1:76-77 is the key to this. "And you, O child (You, O child who are meek, who are humble, who are gentle, who are patient, who are obedient) shall go before the Lord to prepare straight paths, giving His people a knowledge of salvation in freedom from their sins." When we win this battle within ourselves, then we can win it for others as well. We win for them the experience of freedom from their sins. We win for them an experience of salvation, a freedom from that bondage. We win for them the grace to let it go because we're going through the dying process for them.

We need to learn how to handle our own personal anger. Otherwise, how in the world are we going to go through these stages as intercessors, as victim lambs? How are we going to put to death this anger that's going on throughout the world right now if we can't handle the burden that God is placing on each of us individually? We become sin like Jesus did. We enter into His

23

mission with the Lamb to take away the sins of the world. In this tremendous spirit of piety, with the sword and the first word from the Cross, "Father, forgive" we can sever and cut out the root of anger. There will be other days when the anger will come again because we are intercessors, we are burden-bearers, and we are entering into the mission constantly with, in, and through Jesus. We can take on others' unforgiveness so that they can experience salvation through forgiveness of sin. This is the power of intercession. This is what Jesus did for us. Jesus wants to take sin to where the highest form of love is, the Cross, and put it to rest for others now—with, in, and through us.

One of our lay companions drives a school bus. He's dealing with tremendous anger everyday on that bus, but that's his world. Everyday he's dealing with it, and God is showing him different ways to handle it. So we ask ourselves: In *my* world, how am I dealing with it? Am I using the remedy, which is forgiveness and the stages that we must go through? Am I using it for intercession, for the salvation of souls so that others may be set free of that bondage of anger? Our constant model is to behold the Lamb of God who continues to take away the sins of the world in us and through us.

Isaiah tells us, "Come now, let us set things right" (Is 1:18). The words, "Set things right" brings peace. We want things to be right. God is a God of order; sin is disorder. So we want to set things right. We need to ask the Father to consecrate us in truth because His Word is truth. We need His love to cast out fear.

Virtues:
Meekness, Gentleness, Patience

We need to ask for the virtues such as meekness, gentleness, and patience that are needed to fight the capital sin of anger. Each of these witnesses to the Lamb, especially the strongest virtue, meekness. Meekness will counteract anger immediately if we call it forth. Jesus said, "Blessed are the meek. They shall inherit the land" (Mt 5:5). For us, the land is the Promised Land within. Meekness will restore us to that inner peace within. It will restore us to that inner love and presence, into the Kingdom within, into that quietness again, into the presence of God.

Meekness is not weakness. Jesus was meek. Jesus said, "Learn of Me for I am gentle and humble of heart" (Mt 11:29). Learn of Me. Don't learn it out of books. Learn of Me. I am meek and humble of heart. The very essence of meekness is not to cause harm. Meekness will give us the strength not to cause harm and not to act too quickly. However, we can cause harm by omission as well as commission. This is true of all the sins. In other words, the key here is to be submissive to God because the Spirit of Love within us will guide us. There might be times when out of meekness the Spirit might want us to act or to speak, but there will be other times when the Spirit would want us to exert this strength in silence.

In Isaiah 53, Jesus is led like a lamb to the slaughter, and He opened not His mouth. This is tremendous meekness. Jesus said, "It is not to do My own will that I have come down from heaven, but to do the will of Him who sent Me" (Jn 6:38). Meekness is tremendous strength, tremendous restraint. So basically meekness will help us come to that docility, flexibility, and submission to whatever way the Spirit is guiding us. This is why it's so important to take our emotions to the Lord so we can get direction from Him.

Jesus said, "Blest too are the peacemakers; they shall be called sons of God" (Mt 5:9). When we are angry, we are not at peace. Children go through the terrible twos with their little tantrums, stomping their feet whenever they don't get their own way. Often the root when we get upset or angry is that we are not getting our own way, this is not the way we think, or that's not the decision we would have made. It's usually something to do with my will, not God's. So this conversion process, to become a child, is extremely important so that this Beatitude can become alive within us, and we will have that peace. Spiritual childhood is key to our identity. If we listen to Jesus as Our Lady said, "Do whatever He tells you" (Jn 2:5), these virtues that were manifested in Jesus will be given to us as well so that we can do whatever He tells us.

Additional Helps

I believe journaling, or taking our feelings directly to the Lord and dialoguing it out with Him as quickly as possible, is a helpful remedy. As soon as we are in touch with our feelings, we want to hear from God. Our emotions are in the light then. They are not going to be totally solved or dissolved, and we're not going to be totally healed, but it's the beginning of healing because we're bringing it into God's light.

As with any examination of conscience,
begin by recalling God's tremendous love and mercy for you.
Place yourself in the Lord's presence and allow Him
to fill you with His deep love for you.
Rest yourself upon His heart and be at peace.

EXAMINATION OF CONSCIENCE—ANGER

Emotions
In general, am I inclined towards anger?
    How does anger show up in my life? How do I express it?
    Do I often have outbursts of anger? If so, what is the trigger?
    In what situations am I tempted to think angry thoughts?
    Is the anger I feel a holy anger (concerned about God's honor
        and glory) or a sinful anger?
    In what situations is the anger I feel too strong for the
        situation?
    Do I say things in anger and impatience?
    When I feel impatient, what usually happens next?
In what situations do my feelings of anger hinder my ability to
reason?
When I feel some injustice has been done to me or to another, do
I feel the desire to restore the right order through revenge?
    When my ego has been hurt, do I feel the need to strike back?
    Do thoughts of retaliation bring delight?
How can my feelings of anger be a positive force in my life?
    In what ways can I improve the way I handle my anger?
Where do I need to forgive but am holding onto my feelings of
anger?
Are any of my feelings of anger leading me down the dangerous
pathway to hatred?

Relationship with the Lord
Where is my anger bringing about a wicked sadness and
weighing down my soul?
Do I feel that the Lord has let me down and not met my needs in
any situations?
    Is there any buried anger at God for something that has
        happened in my life?
    Am I journaling all my feelings of anger and resentment?
    Am I afraid to tell God how I feel?
    How do these feelings of anger and disappointment with God

cause me to run from solitude and intimacy with Him?

As the Lord is purifying me, are there any areas in my life where I feel deprived?

   Am I afraid to let go of any of my attachments?

   Have I talked to the Lord about these feelings of fear and
      deprivation yet?

What is my attitude during times of desolation?

Do I frequent the Sacrament of Reconciliation to help me deal with my anger?

Relationship with others

Do I have a quarrelsome attitude?

   Am I only pleasant and agreeable with the people I like?

   Has my anger led me to quarrels, insults, abusive words, or
      physical attacks?

   In what situations am I consistently unreasonable and difficult
      to get along with?

Do I treat others with a dignified coolness and give them the cold shoulder when I am angry?

On what occasions does anger start to bubble up within me?

   What do I do then? Do I blow up quickly and without thought?

   Before I react, could I bring this situation to the Lord for His
      point of view?

Am I critical of others, their work, and their accomplishments?

Do I insist on giving my opinion on everything and murmur behind others' backs when things are handled in a way differently from how I would handle them?

When do I feel that people have really let me down in my life?

   What can I do to heal these hurts?

When does my anger have a negative effect on those around me?

   What steps can I take to change this?

Do I pray for my relationship with those who stir up feelings of anger within me?

Do I pray for situations that usually lead me to anger?

Relationship with self

Do I become angry and disgusted with myself because of my personal weaknesses and sins?

Am I impatient that spiritual perfection is taking so long?

Does my anger and disappointment in myself manifest itself in anger towards others?

Are my feelings of anger towards myself unreasonable and unjustified, demanding perfection?
Having made resolutions to increase my holiness, do I become angry with myself when I fail to achieve them?

Community and Family Life
How do my actions show I care about the happiness of others?
Do I believe that my disposition towards anger can hurt my community / family significantly?
   Do I care that my anger has a negative impact upon my
      community / family?
   Am I a cause for division within my community / family?
What am I doing to develop a gentle, meek disposition?
Do I treat each person as I would treat Jesus?
Do my actions or lack of actions cause another to fall into this sin of anger?

The ministry of intercession
Do I critique another's every prayer?
When I am praying for another, do I have a judgmental, superior attitude? Do I judge the sinner? Do I love the sinner?
   Am I repulsed by and judgmental of the sins of others?
What is my attitude regarding winning graces for the salvation of souls?
Whenever I feel angry, do I remember to pray for all people who are also experiencing anger?
Do I view meekness as weakness or strength?
How is my spiritual journey helping me to embrace Isaiah 53, "The Suffering Servant"?

You should be able to see a pattern that is developing regarding how you are susceptible to anger. In general: Do I have a problem with anger? In which situations do I find anger welling up inside of me? What is the root of this anger? Am I taking the time to journal my feelings out with the Lord?

Journal these questions and thoughts with the Lord. Choose one or two areas in which anger seems to be the biggest problem. Create a plan showing the steps you are going to take to help you better resist this capital sin of anger. Pray for a deeper trust and confidence in the Lord. Pray for a holy hatred of this sin of anger.

Chapter 2

Envy

St. Iranaeus said that the glory of God is man fully alive. I just love that definition of God's glory. We want to be fully alive with God's presence within us. We want to be totally transfigured, to be full of life, full of love, full of grace as Our Lady was. The sin that we want to talk about that can block this and can also give the enemy entrance is the sin of envy. That's a big one.

There are many definitions of envy, but basically, envy is desiring something I don't have, I can't have, or I wish I had. For some reason envy is hard to spot. It's hard to put a face on envy. Our Catechism tells us that when envy wants to cause serious harm to anyone, then it becomes a mortal sin (*The Catechism of the Catholic Church,* 2539). Once again, we cannot directly control the rising of an emotion in our hearts. But it is that second step of what are we going to do about this emotion or feeling once we get in touch with it that determines whether we are going to sin or not sin.

St. Thomas Aquinas tells us that "envy is sorrow or sadness over another's good because that good is regarded as something withheld or taken away from the envious person's excellence or reputation" (*A Tour of the Summa,* 36-1). We feel deprived of something that we want or desire, and we have a sorrow or a sadness that somebody else has that. We can be envious of someone else, of their reputation, their friends, their health, their good looks, or their popularity. It could be anything. Basically envy is a sorrow or sadness over somebody else's good.

Several years ago a priest sent a young man to us for prayer ministry. This young man felt that he really should be female. He was absolutely convinced of this and wanted to have surgery. We didn't know how to pray for him, but then we don't really know how to pray for anybody! So we just asked the Lord, "How should we pray for him?" So the Lord told us, "Ask him a question about his early childhood. Ask him what it was like, and you're going to hear what you need to hear." So the Lord didn't tell us directly, but He was going to speak to us through this young man.

So we asked him about his early childhood. He said that he was born out of wedlock and never knew his biological father. As a little toddler, he didn't know that. When he was about three years old, his mother married, and so he always thought that this man was his biological father. After they had been married for about a year, they had a little baby girl. This is when the Lord started to anoint what he was saying very powerfully.

We said, "How did you feel about your little baby sister?" He said, "Well, at first I think I was really jealous of her because she got so much attention and was shown so much favoritism by my father." The reason was probably because this was his biological child, but of course, he didn't know that. So this little four-year-old boy, just a tiny tot, put it together in the non-rationale that if he were a girl, he would be loved like that, too. This is when an actual spirit came into him to convince him that he could become a little girl, too, and get all that love and attention just like his sister. So from that day on, he grew up with this spirit within him telling him this lie over and over.

Once we had this knowledge, the ministry was very simple. First of all, we took authority over that spirit of envy. The spirit didn't want to go because he had been very comfortable living within this person for some time. So the Lord said, "Take him through the way I created him and see what happens." So we did. So we tried to image in how God would create this little baby boy, and when we got to the genital organs, this is when he stood up and screamed, "No, you're wrong. I wasn't created that way. I was created a little girl." Quietly, without verbalizing anything, we had a team take authority over the spirit of envy because we knew the spirit within him was rising up to block the ministry. We just bound that spirit and told it to be quiet.

Then the Lord said, "Do it again. This time it will be different." So we went through how God put him together, and this time it was peaceful. The spirit left because truth had come now. It was one of the simplest deliverance ministries I've ever seen. In fact by the time the ministry was over, we were all singing, "Our Father who art in heaven." He was praising and thanking the Father for making him a male because that would allow him to be more like Jesus. He was totally healed. This is the power of envy. We never know what door is going to open within us. It seems like envy is a special vice of the devil's. He loves to use this particular sin of envy to get to us.

Envy has its own profile, and its own personality like all the sins do. Envy will reveal itself in discord, hatred, malicious joy, backbiting, rudeness, jealousy, bitterness, accusations, rivalry, and competition. It will manifest itself as sadness or coldness at someone's success or joy at another's failures or faults. If envy is at work within us, we can easily misjudge or misinterpret another. Envy will manifest itself in hatred. Now remember that anger manifests itself in hatred, too, but it takes longer in the sin of anger to get to a level of hate. In the sin of envy, we can get there almost instantly. In envy we can almost instantly hate who someone else is or what he or she have. It's not a very pretty sin, yet we inherited this, and it will show its ugly head in many different ways through many different disguises.

Envy is the one sin that brings its own punishment. It poisons and torments a soul so much that it can bring a spiritual death to that soul. Envy is its own punishment. The fruit of envy will bring about a spiritual death in relationships with another person, within myself, and it might even bring about death in my relationship with God. That's how strong envy is.

Jesus said many things about envy, but I will quote only a few things here. First of all, He is very careful to tell His followers (often He is talking to the scribes and Pharisees) not to be envious of God's mercy, particularly to the lost sheep. I've heard stories of people who have resented the Catholic Church giving the Last Rites at the very last moment to public sinners after the way the person had lived their life. It's almost like they are envious of God's mercy, even on a deathbed situation. And yet the good thief stole heaven at the last minute.

Jesus' story of the prodigal son is a good one to ponder. The elder brother was envious that the prodigal son was going to receive all that inheritance. He was particularly envious of his younger brother's relationship with the father. He had worked so hard and had been faithful, and his younger brother had gone off and spent all his inheritance. That's envy. Have you ever felt envious that someone inherited the Kingdom of God at the eleventh hour when you've been working for the Lord for forever? They come right along and at the very last minute they get all these graces and benefits. We may ask, "Why did You do that, Lord?" This is envy.

Jesus said we should not be envious of wealth (see Mt 6:19-21). We see a lot of envy of wealth in America. We might see it in our lives, too. We might see envy over the wealth of other people's gifts, their talents, their strengths, and their relationships. It can come in so many ways.

We have to check our spirit and our hearts. Do any of these categories of envy fit me? Only the Holy Spirit can show that to us. Envy is a deadly sin. It attacks our relationship with God. Satan knows his way around in this sin. This is one of the heads of the dragon mentioned in the book of Revelation and it's strong.

It wasn't until I started praying about envy that I realized that it was envy that Satan used to tempt Adam and Eve to disobey and sin (Gn 3:1-14). This is why he got her. It wasn't that he wanted the relationship they had with God, but he came to destroy their relationship with God. The fruit of this envy was that it severed their relationship with God—not forever, not permanently, but tremendous damage was done. Satan was envious of their relationship with God. Envy attacks our relationship with God.

The first murder committed was Cain killing Abel because he was envious of Abel's relationship with God. Abel had found favor with God. Cain killed Abel out of envy (Gn 4:1-11). Envy entered into Saul. Scripture actually says an evil spirit entered into Saul. Saul then tried to kill David because he saw David's popularity. Everyone was acclaiming David when he came home with the victory. They were dancing and shouting, "Saul has slain his thousands, but David his ten thousands" (1Sm 21:12). So Saul had his thousands, David had his ten thousands. That's jealousy, and from then on, David was a hunted man. Saul hated him; he felt threatened by David. In the story of Joseph and his brothers, it was envy that prompted the brothers to kill Joseph because they were jealous of Joseph's relationship with their father from the very beginning (Gn 37:1-28).

There is a mystery in this particular capital sin, but when I was praying it through, I kept coming up with a triangle all the time. Often there was a third party involved. For example, the brothers were envious and wanted to put Joseph to death, but it was because of his relationship with the father. It's like the person who gets caught in the middle is the person who they want to kill. It's interesting that envy constantly takes us into a triangle. It was the same way in Cain killing Abel. Abel was the one who got killed, but it was because Cain was jealous of his relationship with their Heavenly Father.

One time when I was praying about Jesus being tempted in the desert, the Lord showed me that Satan was there using envy for the temptations. Envy is a powerful sin. It will always try to attack our obedience because disobedience brings death instantly. When I say death, I mean that it separates us and brings death to the relationship. It's a powerful strategy.

When we look at the three temptations of Jesus, we see how envy was attacking and tempting Jesus to sin. "Command these stones to turn into bread" (Mt 4:1-4). In other words, "I can give you all this power." And yet Satan was envious of Jesus and trying to tempt Him into this power act. Power is a tremendous temptation. Power is what many people are envious of. This is what most people want. Satan assumed Jesus would want this kind of power. From the point of view of envy, we see why this was such a powerful temptation.

The second temptation is when Satan talks about the misuse of gifts and tries to get Jesus to misuse His Sonship, to misuse His relationship. "If you do this and this, it's okay because the angels will take care of You if You really are the Son of God." Remember that temptation? "If you are the Son of God, throw yourself down. Scripture has it: 'He will bid His angels to take care of you' " (Mt 4:5-7). Through envy Satan was trying to destroy Jesus because of His relationship with the Father. Of course the angels could have taken care of Jesus. They can take care of us, but Jesus knew that it would not be the Father's will. He knew it would harm His Sonship with the Father, His being that child, His being obedient. It's amazing how Jesus saw through the envy and Satan trying to bring death to His relationship.

In Jesus' third temptation, "The devil then took him up a very high mountain and displayed before him all the kingdoms of the world in their magnificence, promising, 'All these will I bestow on you if you prostrate yourself in homage before me' "(Mt 4:8-9). Satan was promising Jesus the honor and prestige of the world. Look at the temptation that was! People sin because they envy things of the world. They envy people who have riches, whatever those riches may be.

Satan uses envy to make us imitate his rebellion and disobedience so we will also undergo the separation from God. Theologians tell us that pride is the father of envy. Pride is totally opposed to humility, whereas humility is the fruit of obedience. An obedient person will be a humble person. A humble person will always be an obedient person.

St. Paul tells us, "Let us never be boastful, or challenging, or jealous toward one another" (Gal 5:26). The glory of prayer warriors is the presence of God, when we are fully alive with God's life.

What Envy Looks Like in Me

We need to constantly check and watch the movement of our hearts. We need to listen and be sensitive to those feelings to see, "Where are they leading me now?"

This deadly sin will destroy the silence within us. It will churn everything up within and destroy the silence. Satan wants to destroy the silence and peace within us because this is his way of separating us from our relationship with God. Have you ever gone into prayer churning inside, and you come out of prayer still churning inside? Nothing was resolved; nothing was healed. There was no connection with God because you never got out of yourself. You were all wrapped up in this envy. So we need to ask ourselves, "How does envy destroy the silence within me?" Envy can create a lot of noise within us and put the peace within us to death.

Envy will try to show itself through other people receiving honors, recognition, power, and praise. Watch for those little feelings of envy that pop up: "Why didn't anybody compliment me? Why didn't anybody even recognize me?" We can feel envy when we see someone who is very popular or is climbing the social or corporate ladder.

Envy will also try to show itself when we see someone who is very prayerful or more prayerful than I am. It's amazing how envy can rear its ugly head! Or if we see someone with more virtue than we have, consistent virtue, we can feel envy. Maybe they are consistently nice, consistently patient, consistently very kind, and consistently turning the other cheek. Or maybe we feel we don't even like their goodness because they're just too good. "How do they do that?" We may know some people who are very humble. They're very childlike, and they're very free. It's amazing how these people can create enemies because of their holiness. Envy will try to show itself when we see others who love God, who are faithful to God, who are receiving favors from God, and who are just too good.

One time in the cloister I didn't realize I was going into this sin of envy, but as I look back this is what it would have been. In the novitiate I saw other novices receiving tremendous favors from the superior. By that I mean privileges to do things they could do. I didn't get those permissions. At first I thought it was just my imagination, that she hadn't realized that she forgot to give the permission to me as well. After a few weeks I began to put it together that it was deliberate. I became envious, particularly when a priest would come to the cloister and say an extra Mass. This was a special time for cloistered nuns. They could leave their work wherever they were and go participate in that Mass. That is, everyone except me. I was never notified that the sisters had gone to chapel or that I could leave my work in the greenhouse. So later I would hear about this wonderful Mass that the sisters had been to and the wonderful homily they had heard. It was very hurtful.

Envy could have set in right away; it was the beginning of that but I took it to the Lord right away. I went out behind the chicken house, sat there, and cried because I was being left out. I started to complain to the Lord, "Lord, she doesn't treat me like she treats the other sisters." He very gently and lovingly said, "No, she doesn't, but then, neither do I." So get to the Lord quickly.

Envy will try to keep others from being holy. It will encourage others to disobey, to gossip, to lie, to cheat, and to conceal. If anyone is trying to encourage us in any of these ways that are disobedient, then we know we are dealing with envy, and oftentimes the spirit of envy itself.

Envy wants us to fall. Envy wants us to fail. Envy will always want us to disobey. Envy will always try to put virtue and our relationships with others and the Lord to death. God wants us to be holy. He wants us to be perfect. He wants us to be saints.

In My Spiritual Life

Jesus told us not to be envious about not having the first place (see Mk 9:34-35). He is saying, "Don't be envious if you're not the most important person." This is the story where the Apostles were quibbling over who was going to be the greatest. It was very important to them. This "I have to be first" mentality or "Who's going to be the most important?" is envy. The beauty of it is that when the gift of Wisdom is given, then we will see things through God's eyes. We will see that we are important and very special to God, and so we won't need to be envious, but until that gift is given, we can become envious of someone else's place with God.

We can be envious of God's generosity. "Why does God give so many gifts to some people and not to me?" Jesus spoke about envy in the parable of the vineyard where He said directly to the laborers, "Are you envious because I am generous?" (Mt 20:1-16) They were. Remember they had worked all day but the ones who joined on the eleventh hour got the same wages. They didn't like that. They were envious.

When I came home from the cloister, I saw envy in the Charismatic Renewal. God gives people an abundance of gifts, but He doesn't give everyone the same gifts. I was amazed at the envy among the people. "I didn't get that gift. I didn't get the gift of healing. I didn't get the gift of discernment. I didn't get the gift of miracles." It was amazing. This is spiritual envy, and it's deadly.

While our community was doing a formation program on the Capital Sins, one of our members said, "I can't think of anything that I'm envious of. I don't think I have experienced envy." But when she started praying about envy, the Lord revealed, "You are envious of people who have a close relationship with Me." So she said, "Lord, it's true. Why am I envious? What's the deeper root?" God said, "You don't really believe that I love you." She was envious because she thought God loved others more than He loved her. Usually we won't turn against God, but we might turn against the person who, we feel, is the object of God's favor and goodness.

Another member said almost the same thing, "I don't think I've ever been envious of anybody." But in prayer, the Lord showed him, "You're very competitive. You have a competitive spirit. You always have to win. You're devastated when you don't win." He asked the Lord, "What does that have to do with envy?" The Lord said, "You are not secure in My love. I'm not enough for you. It's like your whole self-image is, 'I have to win. I have to win.' You are envious if anyone else wins because you are insecure in our relationship."

If envy truly isn't lurking, then we will be rejoicing that others are holy, that others are good, that others are more prayerful, more obedient, more popular, and more successful than we are. Bottom line, envy always attacks our relationship with God. In Wisdom 2:24 we read that Satan entered the world through envy. Satan actually came into our world through envy, and he is still coming into our world through this sin. He still wants entrance into our house through this sin of envy.

Spiritual Warfare

The evil spirits associated with envy are the spirits of envy, resentment, hatred, self-pity, fear of rejection, judgmentalism, unbelief, self-condemnation, and death. Each will try to sever us from God and others, but we don't always recognize these spirits. As a doctor learns to pay attention to what is moving behind their patient's words, emotions, and actions, we pay attention to any evil spirits moving behind the scenes.

Evil spirits are in isolation because of their hatred, division, and severance from God, yet in their hatred for Jesus Christ, Our Lady, the Church, and Christians, in warfare they will group together. Herod and Pontius Pilate were bitter enemies, but their hatred of Jesus bonded them together. The hatred of these spirits will bind them together.

One of the most common evil spirits holding people in bondage is resentment. Many people are locked into resentment and holding onto grudges, hostilities, and unforgiveness. Whenever we hang onto our resentment and envy, Satan is getting a deeper foothold into us to the point where it will be very difficult to get free of these spirits' influence without special help. It can lead us into tremendous sin if we are not careful. We need to be aware of this and not let Satan even get his little toe in the door.

Remedies

Gift of the Holy Spirit: Wisdom

We need to pray constantly for the gift of Wisdom and not take it for granted. Through prayer, we need to constantly activate the gift of Wisdom because we need to see things from God's point of view, which is quite different from our point of view. We need to know. We need to hear. It's like going up on the wings of the eagle into God's presence in a very contemplative listening posture while a whole panorama comes before us that we couldn't see from our own little inner selves. God's point of view can set us free.

The highest form of wisdom is surrender. Surrender brings about union, which brings about love. If we are totally surrendered to God, we have paradise within us. We have heaven with us. Catherine of Siena realized that heaven itself was within her. If we have paradise within us, there is nothing to envy. We have it all.

In the Book of Wisdom we read that wisdom enters into holy souls and makes them friends of God (see Wis 7:27). When wisdom enters into holy souls and makes them friends of God it means that God has entered into a very special relationship. When we become friends, obedience is very easy because we want to please a friend. Wisdom is the gift that makes us want to say yes to God. It makes us want to do whatever He tells us. Jesus told us, "I have made known to you everything I learned from my Father. I no longer call you servants but friends" (see Jn 15:15). Wisdom is a powerful gift and helps us to combat the sin of envy.

Wisdom is the great gift that Our Lady received at the Annunciation when the Spirit of Wisdom came into her and became enfleshed; it was Jesus. Mary could then cry out that her whole being magnified the Lord and her spirit rejoiced in God. This is the fruit of wisdom: when our whole being is filled with Wisdom Incarnate, when the Word made flesh is enfleshed again and again within each of us in its fullness. As long as we give the Word, Jesus, room to take up His abode within us and make room for this gift to fill us, then we, too, can magnify the Lord in that way.

We can put envy to death when we call forth the gift of Wisdom and beg God to enter into us fully. This day we can enter into that deep, very personal relationship with Jesus, with the Father, and with the Holy Spirit. This is paradise. This is really heaven on earth.

Wisdom brings about a union. The power of wisdom comes in the emptiness, in the surrender, because then God can fill us totally with Himself. It is out of this surrender that union, the fullness of love, comes.

As we allow the gift of Wisdom to fill us, as we surrender and empty ourselves, receiving and making room for this gift as Our Lady did, it will bring us into transforming union. It will bring us into such union with the Word Himself, who is alive within us, that with Jesus, we will become the Sword. Now we have a mighty weapon to battle Satan and all the ways that he enters our world and lives through this very deep sin of envy.

I cannot encourage you enough to pray for this gift of Wisdom. It is a gift that is full of God, full of His presence, full of His grace, and full of His life. It is the gift we receive when we pray the Our Father as Jesus taught us, "Your Kingdom come" (Mt 6:10). "May Your Kingdom come so that there is nothing of Satan's camp or kingdom within me at all, just Your Kingdom and the fruit of Your Spirit."

Words from the Cross

The second word of the Cross, "This day you will be with Me in Paradise" (Lk 23:43), will bring about the victory and put envy to death. The key words are *with Me*. Whenever we are *with* Jesus, we are fulfilled. St. Francis of Assisi said, "My God and my All." When we are with Jesus in this kind of paradise, when we are with Jesus in this kind of union, when we are with Jesus in the kingdom within, what or who is there to envy? We have it all. We are rich, even though others may think we are poor. This is why the second word of Jesus from the Cross will totally put envy to death. We can nail this sin there.

If we surrender with the gift of Wisdom, and if we are humble and obedient, then *this day* we can have that joy and peace and goodness and that presence. We can have paradise this day, this moment. This day—that means now. "This day surrender to My love. Surrender to My gift of Wisdom within. My wisdom is like a spotless mirror. You will see. You will understand. You will reflect my goodness. It will unite you to Me because wisdom produces friends of God."

Virtues:
Love, Humility, Obedience

The main virtue that we need to beg for to combat this sin of envy will be charity, love. Love is a fruit, but love is also a virtue. We will find that these virtues will always interact and dovetail with each other, but the main virtue is going to be love. There isn't any power like charity. This love will be manifested mainly through humility and obedience. The fruit of humility is obedience. So it will always be obedient love.

We need poverty of spirit and emptiness like Our Lady had when she received this gift and said, "The hungry He has given every good thing" (Lk 1:53). The more we can be empty of self, empty of self-love, self-interest, and self-concern, then the more we can be filled with good things as well.

When envy is activated within us, practicing more self-denial will be helpful. We need to pray for an increase in humility and charity. Jesus said, "Blessed are the poor in spirit; the reign of God is theirs" (Mt 5:3). In this full level of surrender, we are in total poverty. We have totally surrendered our lives, our wills, and our preferences into God's hands. When we allow the Spirit to empty us of this envy and fill us with His wisdom, then we know that we possess the Kingdom. In this surrender, the Kingdom, peace, joy, love, presence, and comfort becomes ours. This day, every day, we can be with Him in paradise if we are poor in spirit. One who has the Kingdom within will never be envious of anyone or anything.

The Twenty-third Psalm sums up the prayer for a prayer warrior when they can nail envy to the Cross and be with Jesus this day in paradise. "The Lord is my shepherd, truly nothing do I want" (Ps 23:1). Nothing, nothing do I want.

41

Additional Helps

A practical way to help us counteract envy is first of all to pray. Pray. Get to the Lord quickly and try to see things from His point of view. Tap into His gift of Wisdom, "Lord, how do You see this?" One of the best ways to do this is to journal. We need to journal through all our emotions and feelings, or they can separate us from God very quickly.

Beg for the virtues of humility, charity, and obedience that can counteract envy. Begin to thank God for whatever good is done, no matter who does it. We need to learn to praise Him in all things and for all things; this will start to uproot envy more quickly. We always please God when we accept His will for us, and then follow it. Accepting and surrendering to God's will is the highest form of wisdom, and following it and living it out, as Jesus said, is perfect obedience. This will constantly put envy to death.

So if we find ourselves looking around at what everyone else is doing or what everyone else has or what God is saying or doing in their lives, envy can come in and take us down. St. John of the Cross has a beautiful maxim on always being resigned to God's will for me, keeping my eyes focused on Him and His will for me. It can be difficult to not be concerned about what everyone else is doing, what everyone else has, or what God is asking of other people. St. Peter experienced this difficulty. After the fish fry scene when Jesus said, "Come follow Me, Peter," he turned around and was very concerned about John. So he asked Jesus, "What about him?" Jesus gave us a wonderful antidote to come against this envy when He answered Peter, gently and lovingly, but firmly as well, "How does that concern you? You follow Me" (Jn 21:20-22). Jesus says these same words to us, "You follow Me."

*Put all the distractions of the day aside and
take a moment to place yourself in the presence of the Lord.
Allow His unconditional love for you
to envelop you and fill your heart to overflowing.
Take a moment to recall all the blessings and spiritual gifts
that the Father has so generously bestowed upon you.
Remain awhile in this thankfulness and love.*

EXAMINATION OF CONSCIENCE—ENVY

Daily Life

Do I constantly compare myself to any certain person?
When do I speak of others in a critical way? Where am I judgmental?

Do I treat and judge certain people more harshly than others?
Do I see my brother or sister's hard work and effort, or am I critical and judgmental?
Do I follow the letter of the law or the spirit of the law?

In what situations am I tempted towards envy?
Do I covet anything that belongs to my neighbor?
Am I jealous of other people's talents? possessions? power? accomplishments? intelligence? abilities?
When I am tempted to say an uncharitable word, what is the first thing I do?

What could I do at this time of temptation to help fortify my resolve to be charitable?
Is there something that brings on this temptation?

Is unforgiveness a root of envy in my life?

Do I have difficulty forgiving any particular person's faults?

Do I experience sadness when I see or think about another's prosperity in worldly goods?

Does it make me think less of myself?

Do I feel joy at another's failure or occasion of reprimand?

If so, what am I doing to protect myself from this sin of envy?

Where does envy cause me to not see clearly or love God's presence in another?

When another is being complimented, what are my heart feelings?

Do I rejoice at the success of others?
Is there anyone in particular for whom I have trouble rejoicing at his or her successes?

Do I think less of myself when another is praised?
Do I perceive my cup as half-empty or half-full?
Does my envy ever lead me to wishing harm to another person or situation?
Is my inclination towards envy leading me into the sin of hate in any situation?

Prayer Life
Do I truly see my spiritual gifts as pure gift from God?
  Am I thankful for my abilities *and* shortcomings, consolations *and* desolation?
Whom do I measure myself against? Is Jesus my standard or is it another person?
Do I feel sad when I see or think of another's high degree of holiness, prayerfulness, and virtue?
  Am I envious when another's spiritual progress seems to be faster than mine? Where are these feelings leading me?
When do I experience a holy envy that spurs me to try harder in my spiritual life?
  How am I using this holy envy to draw me closer into transforming union?
Where do I need to trust more fully?
Do I think that God has been "fair" to me?
How does envy destroy the silence within me?
  What can I do to restore the silence?

Community / Family Life
Is my attitude of envy holding another back from progressing in their spiritual life?
Is my attitude of envy preventing unity within my community / family?
How are my feelings of envy harming my community / family? How are they harming myself?
Where do I need to rejoice in another's goodness or holiness?
Am I jealous of another's degree of holiness?
Do I purposely hold another back from holiness so they don't get ahead of me or so I don't seem so bad?
Do I feel threatened when others seem to pass me spiritually?
Is the envy of another whom I perceive as more holy than myself a holy envy, or is it sinful?
In what situations do I find delight in a community or family members' holiness or successes?

Is there an area of uncharitableness within me that is hidden from others' view and is harming my community and family?

Do I show a preference for certain individuals and purposely ignore others?

How do I show that I am my brother's keeper?

Do I encourage community / family members in their area of work? Do I compliment others, including those whom I may be envious of?

Do I use my gifts, talents, abilities, etc., in such a way to make others envious?

Virtues

Where is my charity becoming habitual?

How am I striving to be more humble?

Am I grateful for the many gifts the Father has so generously bestowed upon me?

 How does my gratitude overflow and bring life into all my
 relationships?

 Where do I need to be more grateful?

 What can I do to develop and nurture an attitude of gratitude?

Where is my love too small?

Review the patterns in your life where you are susceptible to the sin of envy. Journal with the Lord about what you are envious of and the reasons why. Allow Him to show you what He sees and the root cause of your envy.

Now reflect on the many blessings the Lord has so generously bestowed upon you. Pause to look at your life with a deep realization that all you have and possess is pure gift from the Lord. Journal these feelings and insights.

In the Lord's presence, compare the things you are envious of with the blessings that you have received from the Lord. Invite the Lord to be with you as you look at both sides. Journal.

Close this prayer experience resting your heart upon the Father's heart and letting Him fill you with His love.

Chapter 3

Lust

Satan attacks us big time through our senses, particularly though the capital sin of lust, which is another one of the heads of the dragon referred to in the book of Revelation. Theologians tell us that sins of lust wrap themselves around all our senses, and then through our senses, enter into our souls. They tell us that lust is the most popular of all the sins (if we can think of sin as being popular). All we have to do is look around our world, and we could say, "Amen" to that. Lust is the inordinate love of the pleasures of the flesh. Lust is seeking unlawful pleasures, especially through the sense of touch. It will come in other ways but especially through sins of touch. Lust is *unlawful* pleasures and is generally spoken of as impurity.

Sins of impurity defile both our soul and body, which is the temple of the Holy Spirit. We are destined at the Resurrection to be in a glorified body, so the body is very important. Jesus chose to become enfleshed in a body, and He continues to choose to be enfleshed now in our bodies. We will never understand that kind of love that He, the Word, the Second Person of the Trinity, chose to become enfleshed in a human body. We will never understand that humility. It's an awesome, tremendous love. We can get lost in contemplation of this.

One day I was kneeling in front of the tabernacle, and I asked the Lord, "Do I have anything that You need?" I was so surprised when He said, "Yes." I asked, "What is it?" He said, "Your body. I have need of your body." Jesus has need of our bodies. He doesn't have any other body here on earth except our bodies now. We are the Body of Jesus Christ here on earth. We really and truly are, and hopefully we are really His mystical body as well. Hopefully we allow divinity and humanity to come into that marriage within us, that wondrous exchange that we speak about at Christmas, "Oh wondrous exchange," when we receive God's divinity and He receives our humanity. We're getting the better deal. God chose to be enfleshed within us.

Have you ever stopped to think how many times we serve our bodies? Our bodies are here to be a servant to us. We are not here to be a slave to them. Many times we get it backwards and become enslaved to our bodies and our senses.

Lust can change the beautiful gift of our sexuality that God has given to us into sin. We are seeing this gift of our sexuality being perverted in so many ways today. A few of the sins committed through lust include adultery (a violation of the Sixth Commandment), fornication, incest, rape, masturbation, birth control, sterilization, and abortion. Today we're seeing sexually transmitted diseases worldwide as never before. We even see women wanting to become men and men wanting to be women. Speaking in reference to these sexual sins, St. Paul said, "Let them not even be mentioned among you; your holiness forbids this" (Eph 5:3). In other words, not even talked about, not even to be thought about, and not even part of your life.

Some of the bad fruit of impurity is it that it blinds our mind, perverts our will, and can bring about a hardness of heart. We can start to rationalize and argue with the Lord that whatever we're doing is okay. The hardness of heart comes when we become insensitive to our conscience and to His will. It can cause an inconstancy in repentance because our emotions will be up and down and all over the place until this insensitivity and hardness of heart become a way of life for us. We will start to compromise, and compromise is dangerous. There is no compromise in God's Kingdom. The more we compromise with God's laws, the more aversion we can have to God. We will start to distance ourselves more and more from Him. It can lead to insincere confessions. We have to be very careful to bring everything into the light. In line with that, lust can lead to sacrilegious communions. It is a very powerful sin.

Impurity fosters an excessive love of the world or things of the world. It can cause mental anxiety through fear of future punishment. I can't tell you the letters we get, at least weekly, of this anxiety of future punishment because of living in sexual sin. Mental anxiety is upon them because they're afraid of the future, and yet somehow they are not able to change the present. I've seen fear take over in some people's lives until they actually run out of church. There's such a fear they can't even go to Mass.

Lust can lead to disobedience, scandal, and total loss of faith. These sins are powerful because we live in the body. This is the body we know, and until we become more and more purified, we're very sensual, earthy, and very familiar with a certain way of life.

Lust is nurtured through idleness, which leads us away from dialogue and communication with God. We've often heard that idleness is the devil's workshop. Lust can be nurtured by excessive attachment to ease, comfort, excessive eating, and drinking. Lust can be nurtured through watching scandalous movies, TV, or sites on the Internet that we shouldn't be seeing. Pornography is everywhere, and it has become a tremendous addiction for many.

What Lust Looks Like in Me

Every day a beautiful prayer is prayed at Mass when the priest says, "Almighty God, cleanse my heart and my lips that I may worthily proclaim your gospel." This is a good prayer to make our own. "Cleanse my lips, Lord. Stop me if I'm saying what Jesus would not say. Stop me if I'm saying something out of habit that I'm not even aware of that Mary would not say. Convict me. Let me feel that anointing from within."

We can ask God, "How is my mind not totally pure?" We may commit sins of lust in our minds through impure thoughts, daydreaming, and lack of attention to the point where all of a sudden our minds are wandering off into areas that can become very harmful to us.

We can ask God, "How is my heart not totally pure?" Obviously, the heart is one of the deeper ways that we can lust and sin through impurity, particularly if our heart is divided or if all human affection is not brought under control. Impure desires and failure to repress them can lead us into serious sin. Remember, we can't always control the first impulse or the first feeling or thought, but it's what we're going to do about it that will either lead us into or away from sin.

Is my heart divided at all? Jesus said, "Where your treasure is, there your heart is also" (Mt 6:21). What is our treasure? What are we trying to hold on to? What feeds us? What is the attachment? Maybe we will find that our hearts are more divided than we realized. Actually, there is a lot going on in our hearts that we don't know about. It is love that purifies the heart. The more we love, the purer our heart becomes.

When I came home from the cloister, people started coming to me with various problems in their lives. I noticed that so many of them were having serious temptations in this area of sexual sin through some form of lust or impurity. As it started repeating itself in so many patterns, I asked the Lord about it. "Why didn't I see more of this in the cloister?" I was not the superior in the cloister, but I was her assistant. When she was ill for two or three months I had taken her place. I had the opportunity to see the sisters one-on-one and to get to know their relationship with the Lord and their trials and temptations, but this sin of lust never came up. So I asked the Lord, "Why?" He said, "Because they loved. They spent all day long loving—loving Me and loving one another. So their hearts were pure." Isn't that interesting?

Sometimes people think, "If I close myself up like a prune and don't get too close to anyone, then I will stay pure." Satan would love that, but actually this is totally opposite from the truth. The more we can reach out, the more we can give, and the more we can love (this is what God wants as long as we are giving His love), then we will become purer. The enemy will try to make us afraid of intimacy.

Often the lack of deep prayer is one of the open doors for lust. People are not experiencing this deep relationship, they are not experiencing being loved, they are not experiencing the presence and touch of God, and so there is a hunger, a loneliness, and an emptiness deep within. They are afraid of these tremendous emotions, particularly sexual emotions, this passion within, and so they are afraid to get too close to God. This is a tremendous strategy of Satan. Often when people are afraid of sin in a sensual or sexual area, the first thing they do out of fear is stop loving. Satan loves that. The more we can love in an orderly way, controlled by the Spirit, the more our hearts will become purified. It is love that purifies our hearts. But again, it cannot be inordinate.

We can ask God, "How are my eyes not totally pure?" Our eyes can be an occasion of sin in this area, giving into curiosity by looking at anything that is impure. A friend of mine from the Legion of Mary used to say to me, "Curiosity is not a virtue." Now I know what he meant. Curiosity is not a virtue as it can lead to a lot of impurity. Today the Internet is a great source of temptation for many people. Our eyes are wonderful gifts, and as with all gifts, they have a flip side of potential vice. The eyes are windows of the soul, but they need to be guarded, or the enemy can come in through our eyes and attack our soul. So we need to regulate what we see and read.

We can open the door for the enemy to get right into our heart and soul through sinful touches. Here the seeds of impure desires are born through our failure to repress the sensations that come from our desires. Desires are powerful. Sometimes we overlook them.

Our ears can be occasions of the sin of impurity through listening to what we shouldn't be listening to, such as off-color jokes, TV programs, or movies. Our failure to stop what other people are saying and our failure to stop what we are saying (but know we shouldn't be saying) can lead us into temptation. Music can be dangerous as it bypasses the senses (even though it enters though our ears) and goes right into our spirit. A good guideline for us is "Are we listening to something that we would listen to in the presence of Jesus or Mary? Is this something He would want to hear? Is it something she would want us to hear?" Oftentimes our answer would be, "I don't think so." We live in a culture where everything is accepted, and sometimes we're not aware that it really isn't pure. It's not good for us, and so we have to restrain what we hear. We need self-knowledge to know what we can or cannot take in.

Our tongue can be an occasion of impurity. The tongue can be a very destructive force, and yet it can also be used to praise God and to lift people and our own spirits. But it can also kill. Again we should consider, "Would Jesus say this? Would Our Lady say this?"

Spiritually, taste is good. "Taste and see how good the Lord is" (Ps 34:9). Believe it or not, taste can also be an occasion of impurity. We can commit sins of impurity through taste by eating to satisfy my appetite instead of eating because I need to eat this to get energy and stay healthy. One of the best ways to counteract this is through the fasting that the Church has so widely recommended throughout the years. Our eating can become the "end" rather than the "means." Once we use anything as an end, then we have replaced God with a created good. So there has to be a certain amount of self-denial. Through our sense of smell, sensual smells or odors can also lead us into temptation.

Our love for others needs to be a spiritual love. It needs to be the love of Jesus, the love of Mary, love with tremendous respect. Excessive familiarity with anyone whom we shouldn't be excessively familiar with leads us into occasions of sin. For example, spouses shouldn't be excessively familiar with anyone of the opposite sex other than their spouse. In the community of celibates like I live in, we should not be excessively familiar with anyone else in the community because of our Spouse, the Lord. If we get into that excessiveness, then we're going to be on the road to severe temptation and possibly sin. Particular friendships, such as singling out certain people that are my favorites, are signs that we could be getting into dangerous areas and need to be very careful. We have to look closely at the companions we choose, the companions our friends choose, and the companions our children choose, as some of these companions may not be healthy for us.

There can be a love of intellectual pursuits. We can lust after that. We can lust after power. A retreat director gave a retreat to priests and was talking about priests getting involved with women. He said to the priests, "Don't be judging your brother priests who are getting involved with women or lusting after them. Many of you probably go to bed every night lusting after power, honor, and recognition." So there are many ways to be impure.

In My Spiritual Life

Lust has a powerful effect on us. It darkens our minds. It weakens our will, which is even more dangerous, because without a strong will we cannot make Godlike choices. Lust blinds us to spiritual values. If we are blinded, then we can't see the light. We can't see truth. If we can't see truth, we are not going to experience freedom. It leads us to place a created good before God. In other words, it doesn't lead us to God at all. It puts God in second or third or fourth place, or maybe in no place at all. Lust puts creation, things, people, and pleasures of the flesh before God.

Theologians tell us that beginners in the spiritual life are very subject to lust because in the beginning stages of the spiritual life they receive a lot of consolations. There are conversions and many graces because God is baiting us. Our spirit receives these consolations and graces as refreshment, renewal, and satisfaction in God. Our senses receive sensory gratification and delight in these consolations. So in our spiritual life, we can begin to hang on to all that gratification. God can give us a beautiful grace to encourage us, but if we keep hanging on to that grace, we can get out of balance to the point where we are seeking self-gratification. Now we're on the border of going into lust. This is where it can open the door for the enemy because he loves to come in if we are starting to have impure feelings or thoughts. It's like the door is open wide for Satan, and then we really will have a terrible struggle. Often these struggles will come in prayer, and the soul often will become afraid of prayer. The soul will back off of prayer out of fear that prayer is going to lead it into sin. That's the enemy. This is one of the reasons we have the dark night of the soul—to purify us from all that is leading us to self-love and self-gratification and into deeper sin.

John of the Cross wrote about these nights of the flesh, the dark night of the soul, and the dark night of the spirit. There are deep recesses in our hearts where we need God to come. Thanks be to God that He cares that much! He'll flash His flashlight around and show us things that we weren't aware of. Sometimes they are so deep within us that He will kind of "put us under" because He's going to do some "surgery." This is a painful process and becomes "a dark night." The consolations and all the things that meant something to us go, and it might be very difficult to pray at this time. This is why we need spiritual directors to help us recognize that this is the dark night and assure us that we are going through the deeper purification now. They can encourage us to surrender to the purification, and the dark night will pass much more quickly.

St. Louis de Montfort said that souls that have a deep devotion and are consecrated to Our Lady pass through the dark night much more quickly than others do. We don't want to stay in the nights very long because with the dawn comes rejoicing (Ps 30:6). One time I asked Our Lady, "Why is it that souls that are really devoted and consecrated to you pass through the nights more quickly?" She let me understand that it's because her whole mission is to say yes to the Lord. She lived out of this fiat. It was such a powerful word that brought Jesus Christ into her body. When she teaches us to say, "Yes, Lord," we are in surrender. We are not fighting the surgeon. Have you ever been in a dentist chair and tried to make sure he doesn't get in too close? When we're surrendered and not fighting God, He can work very quickly. Our Lady shows us and gives us the grace to surrender because she's Lady Wisdom. Surrender is the highest form of wisdom. We go to Our Lady and beg for the grace to surrender to whatever way God is calling us into deeper purification.

Our sin and sinful natures don't only affect us; these affect others as well. St. Augustine said, "Man cannot live without joy; therefore when he is deprived of true spiritual joys, it is necessary that he become addicted to carnal pleasures." So if we don't attach to God and His love, we are going to attach to other loves that we call addictions. We live in a world that is very addicted to carnal pleasures because the world is not entering into an experience of joy with the Lord. There is a lot of immorality and promiscuity in our society that is treated as normal. Many people no longer know the norms of moral behavior. Theologians tell us that if lust ceased tomorrow, we would be plunged into the greatest economic depression in history. We live in a society where almost everything, such as movies, television, clothing, has to do with sex or lust in some form.

We can take our passions and all our emotions to Jesus because they came from Him in the first place. No one is more passionate than Jesus is. I'm conscious of this so much at Mass when the priest holds up the Body of Jesus and says, "This is My Body . . . Do this in memory of Me." Jesus said, "This is My Body to be given for you" (Lk 22:19). We listen to His words at the consecration, craving intimacy with us, "This is My Body to be given for you." Then we receive Jesus' Body and Blood. This is intimacy at its best. We can say these words back to Him—"This is my body now which is being given to You and to Your service for the Father's greater honor and glory."

God is not afraid of intimacy. He is calling us into intimacy, which will close the door to the enemy trying to come in with his lustful intimacy. God is an intimate God. He wants a passionate relationship with each of us.

Spiritual Warfare

Lust wraps itself around all our senses and through them evil spirits can also enter our soul. These spirits of lust, defilement, perversion, vice, larceny, deception, and fear of fears are nurtured by idleness, by attachment to ease and comfort, and by excess in eating and drinking. Also obscene and suggestive literature, scandalous movies and TV programs, immodest clothing, and companions may lead us into sinful actions.

It is one of the penalties of Original Sin that these struggles against impurity continue throughout life and demand a constant custody of the senses, thoughts, desires, and speech. The spirit of penance and self-denial, frequent recourse to the Sacraments, docility to the Holy Spirit, and prayer are the most necessary means to be employed as weapons in this battle. In this way, with humility and self-distrust, we can "fly" even from the occasions of sin.

Remedies

Gift of the Holy Spirit:
Fear of the Lord

We are constantly given an opportunity to choose. When we choose a spouse, we are choosing to reject all other women or men in our lives. When we choose God, we are choosing to reject all that is not of God. This is why the gift of the Holy Spirit of Fear of the Lord is especially operative here. Fear of the Lord is the beautiful gift of the Holy Spirit—the deep hatred for sin and fear to displease God in any way. In other words, we choose to put Him first. "I choose You first." That's what He said, "Seek first His kingship over you, His way of holiness, and all these things will be given to you besides" (Mt 6:33). It's our choice. Scripture tells us that the early Church increased in numbers (see Acts 16:5). They grew out of and were built up through the gift of Fear of the Lord.

Through this awareness of and hatred for sin, we will choose, like Jesus, to do only what pleases the Father. It will set us apart to go forth into battle with the woman who is clothed with the sun, clothed with the Son. We hate sin because of our love for God. Wisdom has given us such a love for God that we have a fear of doing anything to hurt Him. This is how we are with people that we love. There isn't anything that we deliberately want to do to hurt them. We have a fear of hurting them. It's a holy fear.

Scripture says, "The beginning of wisdom is fear of the Lord" (Ps 111:10; Prv 9:10; Sir 1:12). The middle and end of wisdom is Fear of the Lord also. This gift of Fear of the Lord will begin to strengthen us with such a hatred for sin that will begin to uproot all the avenues and areas of lust in our lives. This gift helps us to spot sin, to hate it, and to have the power to do something about it. It's a tremendous gift.

Words from the Cross

One of the main safeguards against lust is the third word from the Cross, "There is your Mother" (Jn 19:27). Our mother is a tremendous safeguard for purity! Through her Immaculate Conception, her total freedom from sin, she is calling us more and more to be reborn into sinlessness and to have sin uprooted within us. This doesn't mean that the temptations will cease; they won't. This doesn't mean that the harassment of the enemy will cease; it won't. But it does mean that the temptations won't be able to influence us as they have in the past. We need to run to her because she is the Immaculate One; her heart is an immaculate heart. She wants to share every grace that she has received from God with her children. She will do it if we allow her. She can fill us with hope if we can really behold her, go to her in prayer, and behold her beautiful immaculate heart and her sinlessness.

We can behold Mary as she moves through the Gospels, particularly on Calvary. We call her, "Refuge of Sinners." Anyone can go to her no matter how sinful they are, and purity comes. Mary Magdalene was purified by her excessive love of Jesus, and so she was there at the foot of the Cross beholding her Mother as well.

"There is your Mother. I'm giving her to you. She's the Immaculata. She has the promise from God of the victory over

Satan. She's pure. She's sinless. Behold your Mother. Take her into your heart as John did, and Satan will not come near you because it is the pure of heart who see God. Behold your Mother."

One time five of us were traveling through Europe and were about to enter Lourdes. I was driving and became conscious that there was a rhythm going on in my heart to the click of the wheels. I heard the Latin words, "Sed libera nos amalo. Sed libera nos amalo. Sed libera nos amalo." I thought, "What in the world does that mean?"

As soon as we got to Lourdes, I asked a priest, "What do these words mean?" He said, "They mean, 'Deliver us from evil'." I wondered, "Why would God be putting those words in my heart as we are approaching Lourdes? Lourdes is a healing place. There are crutches and wheelchairs left there all over the place. It seems like everyone who goes to Lourdes comes away healed in some area of their lives whether physically, mentally, spiritually, or emotionally. There's always some healing grace." Then the teaching started to come because this is where Mary identifies herself as the Immaculate Conception. "O Mary, conceived without sin." The healing of Lourdes and the healing that we all need is the healing from sin. The sickness of the whole world that God came to heal is sin sickness. The Trinity kept saying over and over, "Sed libera nos amalo." "This is the healing I want." God chose His Mother to come into our lives, to come into our hearts, if we but let her, so that we can come against this sin of lust in the many ways it manifests itself. We can begin to uproot lust because we have the power then of the Immaculata to throw out all that is not pure.

St. Louis de Montfort said, "The Most High, with His holy Mother, has to form for Himself great saints who shall surpass most of the other saints in sanctity . . . These great souls, full of grace and zeal, shall be chosen to match themselves against the enemies of God . . . They shall be singularly devout to our Blessed Lady, illuminated by her light, strengthened with her nourishment, led by her spirit, supported by her arm, and sheltered under her protection, so that they shall fight with one hand and build with the other" (*True Devotion to Mary*, 47-48). St. Maximillian Kolbe said that the Immaculata alone has the promise of God of the victory over Satan. This is a powerful prophetic word that speaks right to our hearts. Mary is center stage. Maybe this is why she has appeared in so many different places throughout the world this past century with her beautiful prophetic word straight from heaven.

We go again to Jesus' words from the Cross, "There is your Mother" (Jn 19:27). The disciple took her into his heart; may we do the same.

Virtues:
Chastity, Temperance, Modesty

The virtue of chastity is a beautiful virtue that regulates our basic desires. The psalmist encourages us to strive to become whiter than snow (see Ps 51:9). We can ask God to make us whiter than snow, and this virtue of chastity will do it. One of the fruits of chastity is that our heart will not be divided, and so we can truly keep the First Commandment to love God with our whole heart, whole soul, and whole mind.

There is a very special vision of faith in the purity of heart that sees God in everyone and in the events of life. For those who are living vows of celibacy or celibate lives, chastity brings about a better marriage relationship with the Lord. It brings all of us to a mountaintop experience. In the Psalms we read, "Who can ascend the mountain of the Lord or who may stand in His holy place? He whose hands are sinless, whose heart is clean" (Ps 24:3-4). Chastity will definitely lead us to the mountaintop, to the very summit of intimacy with God.

Everyone isn't called to be celibate, but everyone is called to be chaste. All of us are called to live chastity, to live chastely, to live purely. Married people must also observe chastity through practicing a reasonable self-control. So whether it is the chastity of consecrated priesthood or religious life, or it's the chastity of the single person, or the chastity of wedlock, we must see it all as a dedication of our power to love to the service of God. Jesus said, "Blessed are the single-hearted, for they shall see God" (Mt 5:8). What a motive He has given to us for wanting purity of heart! First of all, He said, we're blessed. We're happy if we have pure hearts. He wants us to have pure hearts. He wants us to be happy here in this life and even more, He wants us to have that vision of seeing Him. Pure hearts can see God. The whole world becomes a cathedral to pure hearts. They see God in people. They see God in events. They see God in animals. They also see where God isn't. So this purity of heart is a tremendous gift.

Another fruit of chastity is purity of intention. Our motives will become more and more pure. Not just what we do, but the reason we're doing it begins to become very pure. The reason we are doing things is for the Lord and not for self. Two people can do identical jobs. One may have a pure motive and do it for God's greater honor and glory, while the other one may be doing it for their own honor and glory. If we can be mindful that we are temples of the Holy Spirit and beg God for the grace of purity, we will become pure much more quickly. He's given us a beautiful opportunity to become beautiful temples filled with His light, His love, and His purity.

Our Lady has told us more than once, particularly at Fatima, "In the end, my Immaculate Heart will triumph." Her immaculate heart, her pure heart, will triumph in each one of us as our hearts become more pure. One time Bishop Fulton Sheen remarked that Jesus is like the red rose on the Cross, and Mary is the stem. Together they are the flower. He said the thorns are the things that will keep us away from impurity. The thorns actually can shield us from all that might disturb or influence our union with Jesus and Mary. So thorns can be used for good as well. This higher love will entail the Cross. As we can stand there with Mary at the foot of the Cross, we can look to the One on the Cross.

We are putting on the breastplate of righteousness and sinlessness, and so we will triumph in this purity of heart. Then we will see God, and we will see God in one another. We need to pray for this virtue of chastity.

Temperance will bring about tremendous modesty and restraint. It will bring mortification of the senses. When our senses are not mortified, they leave open doors. Temperance will brings about a balanced sexuality within us.

We are seeing more and more immodest clothing today. At Fatima Our Lady spoke specifically about the immodest clothing, particularly of women, that was leading many people into sin areas.

We were out at a shopping mall the other day, and I don't think I have ever seen such immodest clothing in my life—and in broad daylight! We were in the stores and someone would go flitting by, and we would just stare. We almost forgot what we were shopping for! Right here in our own city, I couldn't believe the clothing. When we got back into the car, we just stared. It was like being in New York City for the first time and looking at all the skyscrapers. We were dumbfounded. We can see lust working very busily through all the immodest clothing.

Additional Helps

One remedy to help us counteract lust is to find a higher love. If we're drawn to things that are sensual in a disordered way, we can fight it all we want, but it's easier if we try to shift the focus onto a higher love. St. Bernard said that if we want to wean someone from sugar, feed him or her honey. It's sweeter. Don't focus on the sugar or the fact that you can't do this or have that. Feed on honey. So if we're struggling with something in our earthly nature, the pleasures of the flesh and false loves, then let's seek a higher love. God said, "My friend, come up higher" (Lk 14:10). He wants us to come into a pure love, a true love. He wants us to come into honest-to-God intimacy, into a Heart-to-heart relationship with Him.

As with all the sins, it always comes down to our choice. This is the hard part. It's always choice. We are incredibly free to choose. God is always encouraging us to choose life, to choose Him. When Jesus became man He had choices, too. He, the sinless One, came into a very sinful world. He had a free will, too, and had choices put before Him at all times. He always had to choose if He was going to remain sinless. There is a tremendous detachment that is asked of us in the choices we make.

Jesus told the scribes and Pharisees that the tax collectors and the prostitutes were entering into the Kingdom of God ahead of them. The scribes and Pharisees kept the "law" but they weren't loving. They were not loving each other, and they certainly were not loving and kind to the people. So those who were loving, even though for awhile they had loved in the wrong way, were coming now closer and closer to loving in the right way, and Jesus said, "Tax collectors and the prostitutes are entering the kingdom of God before you" (Mt 21:31). I think that's very hopeful. Just as Our Lady was willing to have Mary Magdalene as her companion at the foot of the Cross, she is very willing to have us there with her now.

So the choice is always ours. We have such a power in our free will, and God will not touch it. Satan cannot touch it either, but he can tempt us to make choices his way. God will put beautiful enticements, honey, we might say, in our paths, as though we were little honeybees. He has us sip from His pollen in His little flower garden. So God and Satan are pulling us in totally opposite directions; they are total enemies. One is trying to pull us this way, and the other is trying to pull us the other way, but neither God nor Satan can force our wills.

God chose to do it this way. I didn't realize that for a long time. When I was a new convert, I used to beg Him, "Why don't You just take my free will? Then I won't have any problems. You make the choices, and I'll just do it Your way. I'll do it because You have my will." I thought, "That's simple." He said, "It doesn't work that way." He is a God of love, and He has chosen to leave us free to choose. That's His nature. Otherwise, if He had our free will, we would be forced to love. When we love someone, we leave him or her free to choose to love us in return. Sometimes I hear parents say to their children, "Go and tell Grandpa that you love him." It's a simple little thing. A child can grow up being forced to love. Maybe the child does love Grandpa but let the child freely choose to tell Grandpa. God is a wonderful Father, and He wants us to freely choose to love and freely choose Him.

*Begin this prayer experience by coming before the Lord
without any feelings of shame or embarrassment.
Allow Him to reveal His deep love for you.
Gaze upon the Lord and contemplate His purity.
Pray for a deep desire to let go
of anything that hinders your relationship with the Lord.*

EXAMINATION OF CONSCIENCE—LUST

Personal habits

Do I have a disordered, inordinate enjoyment of sexual pleasure?

Do I have a tendency towards lust or sexual sin?

Is my love all-embracing, for all people? Is it exclusive? Is it appropriate for my state in life?

Is my love for others a spiritual love, like the love of Jesus and Mary? Where do I have difficulty loving another with a holy love?

Where has my love become hardened and insensitive?

Do I seek joy, relaxation, and recreation that are appropriate to my state in life?

Where do I step outside this boundary?

Do I dress and speak in a modest, pure way?

Do my actions or the way I express love cause another to fall into the sin of lust?

Overt lust

Am I involved in fornication, adultery, incest, seduction, rape, homosexuality, masturbation, or any other deviant sexual behavior?

Do I view pornography?

Do I use birth control contrary to the Church's teachings?

Do I have lustful impulses so strong that it leads me to reject sound reason or restraint?

Does lust cloud, blind, and addict my mind and judgment in any way?

What help have I sought in fighting and healing this sin of lust?

My five senses: touch, taste, smell, hearing, sight

Which sense do I have the most difficulty keeping under control?

What can I do to better regulate this unruly sense?

61

What safeguards have I set up to protect and guard each of my senses?

Where do I allow my senses and feelings to lead rather than allowing God's will to lead me?

Where does my heart, my mind, and my lips need to be cleansed?

My environment

Do I read or watch impure books, movies, etc?

Do I visit inappropriate sites on the Internet?

Is there anything in my home or work environment that leads me towards lust? What can I do to help safeguard me from the sin of lust?

Do I lust after knowledge, honor, power, sports, recognition, or anything else that causes me to take my eyes off Jesus?

How am I protecting my community / family from this sin of lust?

My thoughts

Do I entertain impure thoughts?

   In what ways could my thoughts be more refined and pure?

   Do I allow my eyes and thoughts to wander or linger where they should not?

Where does lust have an open door through my thoughts?

   Is there an area of weakness where lust enters?

How can I bring my thoughts more fully under God's control?

For married persons

How am I chaste in my marriage relationship?

   How is my union with my spouse being drawn into a three-way union with Jesus?

   Where do I need to be more chaste in this union?

How does the way I treat my spouse reflect my marriage vows to love, honor, and obey?

   How does the way I treat my spouse reflect that in choosing him/her, I choose to reject all others?

How do I / we experience the unitive, procreative, and agape love of the Father in our sexual relationship?

   Is our marital love a sign and pledge of spiritual communion?

   Is my sexual pleasure isolated from its procreative and unitive purposes?

How is our sexual relationship balanced and within the limits
of moderation?
Are we in line with the Catholic Church's teaching on
contraception?
Is lust perverting and robbing our Sacrament of Marriage of its
sacredness?
Do I have friendships with those of the opposite sex that are
inappropriate and may be leading me into temptation?

For non-married persons
How am I chaste in my vocation?
Do I have friendships with those of the opposite sex that are
inappropriate and may be leading me into temptation?
Do I go to God to fill any craving for affection or empty space
within me?

In my spiritual life
Do I seek and crave spiritual highs, ecstasies, and extraordinary
prayer experiences?
Do I struggle during prayer with impure feelings, causing me to
give up prayer entirely?
Where is lust cheapening, weakening, and trying to draw me
away from my call to transforming union?
Am I seeking the spiritual love of Jesus and Mary in my
relationships?

Take time to ponder the beautiful gift that the Father has given
you in your sexuality. Is there any area in particular where this
gift is being perverted and robbing you of life? Journal any
insights with the Lord. Allow Him to show you what He sees
when He looks at you, and allow Him to reveal His dreams and
plans for you.

In the presence of the Lord, make a concrete plan of how you are
going to avoid this sin of lust in the future. Pay close attention
to how you will choose to avoid temptation and how you will
react when you encounter lustful temptations. Journal this plan
and put it in a place where you will be able to review it daily.
Pray for the gift of purity. Let His love fill you and let His love
be enough for you.

Chapter 4

Pride

St. Thomas Aquinas tells us, "Pride is the beginning of all sin" (*A Tour of the Summa,* 84-2). Pride is the beginning of *all* sin. Pride is the first sin that Scripture tells us was committed. It was committed by Lucifer. In Isaiah 14:12-15 we get a little insight into Lucifer's pride, "How you have fallen from the heavens, O morning star, son of the dawn." Isn't that amazing? "Oh morning star, son of the dawn." His name is Lucifer, angel of light. We hear that he was the most beautiful of all the angels, and Scripture goes on to tell us, "How are you cut down to the ground, you who mow down the nations. You said in your heart, 'I will scale the heavens. Above the stars of God, I will set up my throne. I will ascend above the tops of the clouds. I will be like the Most High.' " That's a description of pride. This is what pride looks like, and it is epitomized in Satan himself.

Scripture goes on, "Yet down to the nether world you go, to the recesses of the pit" (Is 14:15). It's interesting that when the pride within us tries to scale the heights, tries to climb up and be like God, we go down. But in humility, where we go down and surrender, then God lifts us up on those eagle wings right up to His heart, right to Himself, and He cradles us there as He did Jesus. Pride is a powerful sin. It is the sin that was committed by Adam and Eve through disobedience and rebellion.

Theologians tell us that pride is the father of all sins. It is the summit of self-love. Theologians, saints, and mystics tell us that pride is the sin most hated by God, even though lust is the most frequently committed sin. Scripture talks a lot about this particular sin and its penalty. More than any other sin, we hear God's judgment on this sin of pride, which He punishes very severely. The punishment for Lucifer for his pride was very severe; he had just one opportunity to choose God, and he lost it forever. The punishment of Adam and Eve was severe: total banishment from God's presence. Adam and Eve didn't have the full light and the full knowledge of God as Lucifer did, so they were given another chance. Thanks be to God that second chance has been passed down to us! We get lots of chances. God forgives us and forgives us because He knows we are still blinded, we are still in ignorance. He knows that many times we really don't know what we're doing, we don't know the fullness of our actions, and so we don't receive the full penalty of that sin.

St. Gregory defines pride as "the queen of vices, which conquers the heart of a man and delivers it to the Capital Sins." Pride is the gateway; it's the doorway. Pride interacts with the other sins and has a tremendous influence on how we act, how we pray, how we love, and how we don't love. St. Gregory and St. Thomas Aquinas said that pride is especially the root of spiritual sloth, envy, and anger, and of all the sins, pride is the most dangerous. It blinds our understanding. When we are blind, we can easily stumble and fall. Blindness puts us instantly into the dark. It's spiritual self-delusion. In other words, we attribute our good qualities to ourselves, not to God. We also give ourselves the right to use our "good" qualities any way we like.

In pride we are moving rather independently of God. Pride puts itself first and is totally in opposition to the First Commandment where we are to love the Lord our God with our whole heart, our whole mind, and our whole strength. We are to put God first. Pride will not do that; we place ourselves before God. In other words, we are really saying, "My will be done." Sometimes, we're not just saying it, but we're doing it—"my will, my way." There was a popular song, "My Way," with the words, "I did it my way." It's sad, but pride says that it has to be my way, my will.

What Pride Looks Like in Me

Theologians break pride into a few categories to help us put a face on it. What is its personality? How does it work in me so I can spot it within myself and others? (This is helpful, particularly when we are praying for others and ministering to them.)

Pride of intellect. Pride of the intellect, intelligence. This would be attachment to our own judgments, opinions, and thoughts. "I know it all." If we are proud in our intelligence, then we're going to flee from anyone who has authority because obviously we know as much as they do, if not more. We are not going to act justly if we are operating out of this kind of pride. Scripture says, "Trust in the Lord with all your heart, on your own intelligence rely not" (Prv 3:5). Pride of intellect is basically an unwillingness to learn, to be open, and to listen to God.

The first time I ever read the book of Job, I was so taken with Job's answers. I thought, "My, Job is wise. These are tremendous answers." And then God chastised him about His answers, "Oh so, Job, you know then how the sun comes up and you know how this happens. Well, you tell Me this and you tell me that" (see Jb 38:1-40:2). All of a sudden I saw God's wisdom, God's knowledge, and God's intelligence matched against Job's. Poor Job didn't stand a ghost of a chance! We don't either. It's just that pride doesn't know it, but humility does. Resentment can set in here because pride of the intellect will deeply resent anyone telling them what to do because they already know.

Pride of intellect leads to sins against faith. Faith is first and foremost a gift of the heart, not of the mind. The heart knows. The heart sees. The heart understands. In faith, once the heart knows, sees, and understands, it can relay that information to the mind, and then the mind can execute that information and put it into practice. With pride of intellect, this information never even gets to the heart. The "intelligence" (and I use the word in quotes because it's not God's intelligence) can kill the heart knowledge. It won't even get it to the heart. Knowledge is a gift of God. He wants us to know. It's an infused gift: He gives knowledge to the heart and then the heart conveys that to the mind. Knowledge comes first and foremost from God into our hearts.

But those of us who have pride of intellect only let knowledge come into our minds. It never gets into the heart, and when we do that, we're killing faith. This is what is so dangerous about pride of intellect—faith comes into the heart. It's faith in the heart that knows, that understands, that believes, that loves. Faith is the key gift here and this kind of pride can put it to death. When we see this operating in someone, we will rarely see much faith in that person, if any, because they can't make the journey from the mind into the heart to believe.

In the spiritual realm, pride of intellect can want a higher level of prayer without wanting to go through the process and the stages. When we first got involved in the Charismatic Renewal years ago, everyone was on such a high. It was like a honeymoon. People were hearing from the Lord for the first time. In fact,

everyone would start his or her conversation with, "The Lord said
. . . ." That was wonderful, but I had to smile when I heard them
say, "My, we're in such union now with God. Do you think we're
in the seventh mansion?" I said, "I don't think so. I think it's the
honeymoon stage, but we're on our way."

There is a process in the spiritual life. There are the valleys, as
well as the mountain peaks. There are the nights as well as the
days. It's a journey because it's a purification process. It's a
journey like the one the little caterpillar makes when he's going
into the cocoon. He has to take the risk of dying. He never knows
if he's going to come out. He wraps that little cocoon around
himself. He may be there forever. We never know when the night
is going to lift either, but when it does, look at the freedom! A
whole new life. This little guy who could only crawl on the
ground now can fly. That takes awhile for us; it's a process. But
pride wants to get there right away. Pride wants to scale the
heights and be like God immediately, but it takes awhile for our
fallen nature to get purified and lifted up on those eagle's wings
into union. It doesn't happen overnight.

Pride of intellect is presumptuous. We can presume that "I'm a
child of God," and that's true, but pride of intellect will take some
of that knowledge and presume on it, "Then I can do anything.
God's going to pick me up. God's going to love me."
Presumption was one of the temptations Satan used to try to get to
Jesus to fall, "If you are the Son of God, throw yourself down.
Scripture has it: 'He will bid His angels take care of you; with
their hands they will support you that you may never stumble on a
stone' " (Mt 4:6). That's presumption. We never presume on
God, we never assume, but Satan is constantly tempting us to do
that. One time I asked God, "What is the difference between
presumption and just doing whatever You say?" He said,
"Presumption is walking ahead of me; the other is following Me."
One can lead to death; the other will lead to life and total freedom.
It's dangerous to walk ahead of the Lord. We've all done it
probably. We may think, "Certainly God would want me to do
this." Somehow in our spiritual pride (often that we're not even
aware of), we think that we know the mind of God, so we don't
stop and ask. We just do it, and then we wonder why everything
goes wrong.

Pride of superiority or authority. Pride of superiority can make
us want to control the lives of others. It makes our will rigid and

unbending when others assert authority because we feel we have this superiority. "Don't you know who I am?" Pride of superiority will especially show up when others assert their authority.

Another name for pride of superiority might be pride of independence. This kind of pride is, "I don't need you, and I don't need God to tell me what to do." Have you ever heard people scream that at you? "Don't be telling me what to do." This pride of independence leads us to disobedience, contempt, and contradictions. We are refusing the advice and assistance of others, not even allowing anyone to help us, including God.

It is excessive self-love. It is overbearing and arrogant. It has a very critical attitude. It's bossy, argumentative, conceited, and unkind. It wants no advice and accepts no counsel, not even the counsel of the Holy Spirit. Pride of superiority easily leads us into the capital sin of anger in our thoughts, words, and deeds. It's easy to pass over into severe anger if we're operating out of this kind of pride.

In Jeremiah 35:13 we hear God speaking to the prophet, "Will you not take correction and obey My words?" Nothing has really changed, has it? Human nature is still what it is. What has changed is that Jesus is here, lifting us out of our fallen nature, purifying us, and giving us those wings.

Pride of ambition. This kind of pride seeks positions or places of honor, recognition, and praise for ourselves rather than for others, and it can show up in the tiniest way. Are we the first to grab the food off the table to make sure we get our portion? Pride of ambition wants to assert itself and places itself before others. Jesus talks about this kind of pride at a banquet regarding where we sit or where we don't sit. It has excessive confidence in oneself and in one's abilities. This can be deceptive because we want to have confidence in our gifts and abilities. We want to have a healthy, good self-image. We spend a great deal of time in inner-healing ministry so that people can embrace a healthy self-image. But pride of ambition is an excessive self-image where we are overly confident in ourselves and in our abilities that we go back into that mode of independence. In other words, all we do is not for God's greater honor and glory but for ours.

Pride of sensitiveness. This would be manifested in people who are super-sensitive. They harbor grudges, suspicion, and hostility. They are easily wounded and hurt. If we are very easily hurt, and if someone can just look at us cross-eyed and it hurts, then we need to take a deeper look at why we react this way. We need to take a deeper look because pride is showing itself in our acting overly sensitive.

This kind of pride can pull down the morale of a whole household. It will usually spread bitterness and negativity. It can be like a pall just hanging over a whole family or a community if it's not corrected. It can lead others to speak so carefully so as not to hurt another's feelings. Whenever we do this, we are actually causing this overly sensitive person to become even more sensitive. We are enabling them to continue in that excessive sensitivity which is really a form of pride. So if we can to learn to spot it, we can help the person to grow out of it and become free.

Pride of sensitiveness will be unforgiving because it has a sense of satisfaction in not speaking to others, even for a long term. There is a sense of satisfaction that is feeding this kind of pride, and it can receive a false joy out of feeling badly. It wants to carry ill feelings. "Poor me." Those with pride of sensitiveness refuse to speak to those who have hurt them, and when they do speak, it's very cold.

This kind of pride may hide its pride in self-pity. It's very deceptive when this happens. One time the Lord told me that whenever I withhold love from anyone, I am withholding life from that person. This type of pride can withhold life.

If pride of sensitiveness is manifested in us there is a woundedness over every *supposed* lack of recognition or neglect. I say supposed because it's always how *we* view things in this pride of sensitiveness. We may not really be neglected or overlooked but that will be our perception of it. This kind of pride feels unloved and unwanted, that everyone is against them. This kind of pride is overly anxious of what other people think of me. It has magnified what other people think and will brood over imagined wrongs. Again, they may not be true at all, but it's what the person perceives to be true, and they will brood over these imagined wrongs.

Pride of timidity. Pride of timidity is closely linked with pride of sensitiveness. It comes from an unreasonable fear of other's opinions of us and whether others have respect for us or not. We will even compromise in order to make sure we have someone's respect or friendship. Because of the timidity, we will try to hide our weaknesses and imperfections out of fear of ridicule. Fear is the driving force in this kind of pride. With pride of timidity, we lose strength and courage to keep our resolutions and stand up for what we know is right. We'll vacillate. We're building our house on shifting sand, which limits the way God can use us. We let many opportunities for God to use us slip by because of our fear to step forth and follow the counsels of the Lord.

Sometimes we might think, "Isn't that person humble?" But it might be pride of timidity operating instead. We might think, "If I'm timid, and it looks like humility, then they won't see my imperfections and weaknesses. They won't see that I can make a mistake because I'm not going to do anything to make a mistake." When we're in humility, we don't care if our faults show; we're transparent. We're not even aware of ourselves. Humility is not even looking at ourselves, whereas pride is only looking at ourselves.

Pride of scrupulosity. Scrupulosity has a tendency to fix itself and its attention on the wrong things. We can become very unscrupulous about things that ought to concern us. Pride of scrupulosity diverts our attention. We can get terribly hung-up on scrupulosity while letting the things that really are important, the things that really count, the things that are really quite major go unattended. Jesus spoke to the Pharisees about this very thing when He said, "Oh you Pharisees! Although you cleanse the outside of the cup and the dish, inside you are filled with plunder and evil" (Lk 11:39).

Pride of complacency or vanity. In pride of complacency, we're very self-centered. We're very touchy, easily offended, complacent, and anxious to be well thought of in regard to spiritual, mental, and physical things. We want to be in the spotlight, with the impression that we have everything together. It can be a false sense of perfection.

I used to be a perfectionist, and it was an awful bondage! My superior in the convent caught it and drew it to my attention. God gave me His light to see that I had to have everything in its own little pigeonhole. Everything had to be perfect. If I had to type a letter, and it had one tiny mistake, I'd redo it until it didn't have any, even if it meant that I had to retype the letter over and over. Everything had to be perfect. If I was running something off on the copy machine, it had to be perfect. If I had to get up at three a.m. in order to have more time to do something perfectly, that's what I would do. Perfectionism is a terrible bondage as we want to be well thought of in regard to all areas.

Pride of complacency places a false regard on the opinions of others because we also operate out of the pride of intellect where we already have our opinion, and of course, it's right. It's the best. We might listen to other people's opinion, and we might tolerate their opinions, but we really don't take them to heart.

This kind of pride is very dangerous as it compares itself to others and not to Jesus. We have a tendency to do that. John of the Cross spoke a great deal about not comparing ourselves to others. Sometimes we can look at other people and think, "I'm really doing well. I'm doing much better than they are." But when we look at Jesus, we might see a different picture. Pride of complacency causes us to compare ourselves with others, and therefore rationalize that everything is okay. That's how the complacency comes. "I'm okay. I don't have to change. I have my life much more together than they do." Or, "I go to Mass everyday. They hardly go at all." We can compare, compare, compare and that makes us more complacent. It feeds this kind of pride because we're not focusing on Jesus. The Pharisees had this kind of pride. There's hypocrisy to it. We can be very critical of others and boastful even. St. Paul so beautifully said that he could only boast in the Lord Jesus Christ (1Cor 1:31; 2Cor 10:17).

Pride of complacency can lead us to be overly talkative to the point where we just can't stop. We don't let anyone get a word in; we're doing all the talking. I have to smile sometimes when we're on airplanes. The person sitting next to us will almost talk himself or herself clear across the country. We're just listening, "Mmmm, uh-hmmm, uh-hmmm." What is really humorous is when it's time to deplane, they'll stand up and say, "Gosh, it's really been nice talking with you," and we haven't said a word!

It can lead to lies and contradictions and legalism in our actions. "Well, I'm following the rule. This is what the rule says." Jesus had a problem with the Pharisees' legalism. Often we are caught between the two laws. The Lord said, "I will place my law within them, and write it upon their hearts" (Jer 31:33); it's the law of love. But pride won't go to that law; it will go to the letter of the law. So there is legalism, hypocrisy, and stubbornness in our actions. This is all false humility.

This reminds me of an incident that I saw when I was still in the cloister that illustrates false humility. One of our higher superiors from the provincial house came and visited us. She obviously wanted to practice humility. I think her motive was probably sincere. We were all getting in line for lunch; it was cafeteria style. Because she was the guest, we gave deference to her to go first. But she said, "No, no." She wanted to go last. We said, "No, you're our guest." Well, she actually argued with one of the sisters. As I was standing there watching, the Lord let me see the scenario that was going on. Somehow she thought that because she was so high up that to take the lowest place would be humble, but she ended up making a big scene and drawing attention to herself. It delayed the lunch line about ten minutes. I asked the Lord, "Is this humility?" He said, "No, that's pride. It's a false humility, and it can be deceptive." False humility can happen to any of us when we think we are being humble. Humility is not so much what we do, but it's our childlike attitude of letting others give to us and letting others serve us. It's letting others say, "No, you go first. You're the guest." This cuts right through pride.

One time in the confessional I said, "I can't believe I said that. I don't know how I could have done that. I'll never do it again." I don't remember what "that" was now, but I just couldn't believe I'd said whatever I had said. Right away the priest said, "Well, you're speaking out of pride. That's pride." I thought he was going to sympathize with me, "Oh you poor dear. Whatever made you say that. That's going to be all right. Don't worry." But instead he said, "That's pride. What makes you think you couldn't have said that? With the grace of God, you'll never do it again." If we find ourselves saying, "I'll never do that again," we need to be careful. St. Philip Neri said, "There, but for the grace of God, go I." We need to have the humility of heart, knowing that without the grace of God, we can't do anything. Jesus said, "Apart from Me, you can do nothing" (Jn 15:5). There's a power in humility because we're moving with God.

In My Spiritual Life

Theologians tell us that spiritual pride will turn us away from contemplation of divine things. It urges us to run from those who reproach us, even when they have lawful authority over us and are acting in a just manner. We may even feel resentment towards them.

St. John of the Cross tells us that spiritual pride will show up in beginners. As we become aware of our progress spiritually, our zeal and diligence in pursuing perfection will be increased. The danger lies in that we may start to develop a secret pride, which leads to complacency with ourselves and vanity in our accomplishments. We may begin to condemn others who don't have similar devotions as we do. We may desire to speak of spiritual things in others' presence in order to draw attention to ourselves and our story, rather than focusing on the work the Lord is doing. We prefer to instruct others rather than to be instructed ourselves.

At this point in the spiritual journey, Satan will tempt the beginner to even more fervor for performing spiritual works and devotions, knowing that our real motivation is not for God's greater honor and glory but because "it makes me feel good." In spiritual pride, the hidden focus of everything is self.

With spiritual pride we will be happy with our spiritual directors provided they are telling us what we want to hear. We may begin to hold back information and minimize our faults from them so we don't have to discuss our personal failings. We may want God to remove our faults but our real motive is our own peace rather than God's greater honor and glory. If God were to remove our faults at this time, we would fall even more deeply into serious spiritual pride. The dark night of the soul that St. John of the Cross speaks about helps purify beginners and make us advance more quickly in our spiritual life.

One of the areas where we see spiritual pride displayed is in witnessing. Have you ever heard someone give a testimony of Jesus and when they were through, you really didn't feel you knew anything new about Jesus or understood anything more about Jesus? Maybe you couldn't put your finger on it because it's so subtle. We start to witness about Jesus and then, in our pride, our witnessing starts to focus on ourselves. It ends up as a self-glorification. People hardly realize they are even doing it.

When we read the lives of the saints, we see that they are so afraid of pride because this spirit is very clever. As intercessors, we also have to be very careful because the way the enemy can attack us is very subtle. Suppose we have really, really prayed and fasted and travailed and suffered for something and the answer comes. We get the victory! We have to be really careful that we don't say, "I did it! I knew it was my prayer. I knew that if I did this, I'd get the victory for you!" Have you ever heard an intercessor talk that way? Maybe you have spoken this way yourself. There are times when we can say to someone very legitimately, "God gave me a burden for you. I have been praying for you." People need to know that God has others in intercession for them, but it is when we go that extra step and take the credit for the victory that we have slipped out of God's camp, right into Satan's. Satan will try everything to have us glorify ourselves. Only God takes credit for the victory!

The heaviest burden that gets laid upon intercessors is pride. We are coming against this a lot because this is the sin of all sins. Pride can be manifested in rebellion, anger, spiritual pride, and is part of all the Seven Capital Sins. Pride can be subtle, and it takes tremendous virtue and energies of an intercessor to really be obedient, to be little, to remain hidden and vulnerable when being assaulted by the emotion of pride. When we're carrying the sin of pride, everything within us wants to strike back and be aggressive, terribly assertive, demanding, and obnoxious. This is a very difficult burden to carry for others as it is also very much within ourselves—in our minds, psyches, spirits, and even our bodies. So when we are carrying pride, the load can be quite heavy.

Bottom line: pride is total independence from God and others. All we do is not for God's greater honor and glory but for ours. Pride is always based on Satan, who is the father of lies. We have to be careful of how we think and what we say. Pride will sever us from the Lord and will have a tremendous effect on our intercession for others. There's a Goliath within all of us that we have to constantly put to death with the littleness of a child, with that little Rock (Jesus) that's in David's pouch. He's little. David was humble; he just had a little rock. If we are humble and have the Rock, Jesus, to come against the giant, whether it's Satan or any of his cohorts, we're going to win because we have the power of God. When David had to wind up his arm and throw the rock, he wasn't counting on himself. He knew he had God's power. God gave him the power. God gave him the aim. God gave him the Rock. God does it all for the humble of heart, and we'll win.

Spiritual Warfare

One of the dominant evil spirits that we will run into when we're dealing with the capital sin of pride is the spirit of mockery, but it's repressed mockery. It is very powerful and will manifest itself in giddiness, and excessive laughter. It's a very powerful spirit, and it's concealed. There's an evil spirit of pride, intellectual pride, and self-righteousness. There's a spirit of religiosity which we often bind so that a person's mind can be free enough to get the lights that God wants to give it. There's a spirit of idolatry because we've placed ourselves before God and so the idol is me, myself, and I. There's a spirit called delusions of grandeur, which we'll always find in pride. There's a spirit of lies and rebellion. We see a spirit of rebellion operating very powerfully in the Garden of Eden along with the spirit of disobedience. The spirit that often travels with Satan is what we call the Jezebel spirit. She is Satan's woman. She's the opposite of Mary. She is anything but feminine, and she hates Our Lady. We often encounter the spirit of the antichrist as well.

In this area of pride, we will often meet Satan directly. Not that he can't be directly in the other sins. He is the dragon (as referred to in Rv 13:1). He has the seven heads. He is the father of all sin, but we encounter him especially in the sin of pride. We find that when we're dealing with other sins, he usually sends his cohorts, ministering spirits, and powers and principalities, but it seems that when we're dealing with pride, we come directly against Satan, the head himself.

John the Contemplative tells us that this is what we proclaim to you: "What was from the beginning, what we have heard, what we have seen with our eyes, what we have looked upon and our hands have touched" (1Jn 1:1). They were very careful to witness only to the Lord. So we try to witness with the fruit of what we experience, not particularly how we got there, but we focus more on the fruit. This points right into God's Kingdom, right back to the Lord. Now if we're not aware of this subtle focus on self and this door stays open within us and doesn't get healed, a spirit of divinization may come in and witness. St. Paul talked about this spirit that was in one of the followers who wanted to do what Paul did and kept saying how wonderful it was that Paul had these powers (see Acts 16:17-18). He kept pointing everything to Paul, to the human. This spirit is very subtle. Here Paul is doing this wonderful ministry, but the spirit of divinization is crying out and pointing the spotlight on Paul. Do you see the difference? St. Paul saw it, caught it, and cast it out right away. It is a high-powered spirit, and it will try very subtly to get the spotlight off God, off Jesus, off Mary, off God's Kingdom, and subtly put it on human beings, even the best of human beings.

We read, "no lie has anything in common with the truth" (1Jn 2:21). Every lie is from Satan. Everything about Satan opposes truth, but God's truth opposes Satan as well. So we call upon God's truth quickly because without His truth, without His light, we can't spot the enemy because at this level, Satan shows himself as an angel of light and that light is usually too bright for our natural light. We need a brighter light to see, and so we call on God's light and God's truth, and for His knowledge, wisdom, and understanding.

We are putting on the belt of truth and are keeping it on at all times. It's the belt of truth manifested through the gift of Counsel because we take counsel with the Holy Spirit, who is the Spirit of Truth. We know it's truth. We know that when God counsels us, when God directs us, and when God reveals anything to us, it's truth. We are moving in pure truth. We are moving in light then, and we are moving in power.

Remedies

Gift of the Holy Spirit: Counsel

The gift of the Holy Spirit that is particularly used to counteract pride is the gift of Counsel. It's not that the Holy Spirit will use only the gift of Counsel. He'll use His other gifts as well, but the gift of Counsel is the main gift.

When I was a new Catholic and heard that we were receiving the gift of Counsel in Confirmation, I thought, "Oh that's nice, particularly for people who are in the vocation of counseling. They obviously need this gift. I won't need it because I don't counsel." It took me a couple of years before I began to realize that it's the Holy Spirit who is doing the counseling. We need this gift so that we can take His counsel. It's a beautiful gift.

Submission is needed if we're going to follow the counsels of the Holy Spirit. This is why the gift of Counsel will cut right through pride because Counsel will bring us into submission. Humility cuts through pride over and over.

In Scripture we read, "Let no one deceive you" (1Jn 3:7; 2Thes 2:3; Eph 5:6). The way that no one can deceive us is by simply using this gift and asking for God's counsel, asking for God's opinion, knowledge, revelation, and direction. We go to the very Source of truth and check it out. Even though we have heard from God, we check our discernment out with our spiritual director, and if it's a major discernment, with our confessor. We check it out so that we never move on our own discernment.

The Lord let me understand that this is where Eve really made a mistake, big time, in the Garden. He said simply, "She didn't check it out." Eve couldn't stop the first part of the conversation with the serpent, but she didn't have to fall into his pride. She heard from Satan, she heard the lie, she responded, and she moved on it. She never once went back and asked God, "Is this true? This is what he said. This is what You said," and had it explained. She never once went back to God and checked it out. I find that very interesting. Scripture says that Adam and Eve walked with God every day in light and truth, and yet she never went back and was counseled. Satan will try to get to us that way, too. "Don't check it out." We take counsel from God. We go right to the Source of truth and check it out.

Every time we take counsel with God, we are going more deeply into humility. We're becoming like a child, which is what the conversion process is all about. We are asking God what He thinks, what He knows, and how He feels about a situation. This is why we receive our authority. If God is counseling us, we are operating under His authority. Once we understand what God is asking us to do, then we are moving under His authority. His authority is not only behind us, but we have His authority moving through us. Once we hear from God, we are very sure. Nothing can stop us. Nothing can change us. We are a stronghold. We're on the Rock then. We stand firm. Nothing can change us because God has spoken. This is why it's so important to take counsel and to learn to listen and simply do whatever He tells us. That is authority.

One reason why this authority is given to children is because they know how to ask questions, and they obey. They do what they hear. Scripture tells us, "Let the weak man say, 'I am a warrior' " (Jl 4:10). That's interesting: the weak man, not the strong man. A strong man is pride. A strong man doesn't need God. In fact, Jesus said, "No one can enter a strong man's house and despoil his property unless he has first put him under restraint" (Mk 3:27). When we are weak, then we are strong because then we have God's power, God's presence, and God's authority, and Satan knows it. You will know it, too, by the fruit.

Humility is a beautiful virtue. We can't really see it; we can't really define it because once we think that we're humble, right there we know that we're not! But we do know if we're being obedient. We do know if we are saying yes to the Lord. We do know if we are taking counsel with God. If we are doing that, then it is humility. We are being led by someone else's wisdom, someone else's knowledge, and someone else's understanding. This will crush pride within us.

So this gift of Counsel is a beautiful gift that will definitely give us life and bring us into God's light. It will set us free always from the death within.

Words from the Cross

Jesus' fourth word from the Cross, "My God, My God, why have You forsaken me?" (Mk 15:34) is really the epitome of counsel. When Jesus is dying, covered with our sin, what does He do? He still cries out for counsel. He asked the question, "Why?" No matter where we are in the spiritual life or whatever event is going on, we always must cry out, "Why, God? Show me; teach me; help me." We go to God immediately. Jesus is on the Cross as the Lamb taking on sin, particularly this sin of pride. He is experiencing the total alienation. He's experiencing the fruit of pride right there.

We will experience the fruit of pride when we take on the sin of pride for others. We will experience being forsaken by God but not being abandoned. Jesus did not experience abandonment, but He did experience being forsaken. Deep, deep down we know

God will never leave us because Jesus said, "I will not leave you orphans" (Jn 14:18), but we can experience the alienation that sin causes when we are taking on tranferences of the sin of pride and our own pride as well. We cry out and beg for the humility to always surrender to whatever it is that God wants. Pray, pray for the gift of humility. Pray for ears and hearts to be open to listen and desire God's counsel. The more we can pray for whatever we're experiencing on the cross, the more quickly the grace for others will come, and the transference will be over sooner as well.

It's interesting that a person who is filled with pride will never ask God a question. They're not interested because they already know all the answers. Our approach is, "God, I don't know." Like a child, we don't know. We know that we don't know and that's why we ask.

When Jesus cried out to the Father on the Cross, He came against pride itself when He asked the question, "Why have You forsaken Me?" He cut through pride right there. Pride is independence of God, and it's filled with lies. Humility is total dependence on God which means that we're in touch with our limitations. We really know who we are and who we are not. Calvary is the summit of God's love and the summit of humility as well, while pride is the summit of self-love.

Virtues:
Humility, Obedience, Gratitude

In Isaiah we read, "I am the Lord, your God, who grasp your right hand" (Is 41:13). When I heard that I thought, "I'm a right-handed person. I do everything with my right hand. Lord, if You grasp my right hand, I can't do anything." That's exactly what He wanted me to understand. God's right hand is His hand of power, and our right hand is what we try to use for our own little power. So He said, "No, I'm grasping your right hand," and it was like He read my mind because the next line says, "Fear not, I will help you" (Is 41:13). "I'm going to do it."

I don't think I have read or heard any reading where God uses "I, I, I." In this short reading, He talks about Himself, "I, I" nine times. Now if we say, "I, I, I, I, I" nine times, we know what that is. But God is saying, "I will help you." Then He repeats it again three lines down. "I will help you. I'm your Redeemer. I'm the

Holy One of Israel" (see Is 41:14). He was telling me, "You don't need your right hand. I'm going to grasp it. It's going to be My power. I'm going to do it." "I will make of you a threshing sledge" (Is 41:15). In other words, "I will make you a powerful intercessor. I will answer anyone who is in need. I will answer all your intercession, and I will answer your prayer. I'm the God of Israel. I will not forsake you. I will not forsake them. I will open up rivers on the bare heights, and I'm going to open up my Spirit. I will turn the desert into a marshland. I'm going to put the water there for my chosen people to drink. I will plant in the desert this cedar. I will set in the wasteland the cypress, together with the plane tree and the pine" (see Is 41:13-20). He goes on nine times with all the things the great "I AM" will do while grasping our right hand. And then He says, "That all may see and know, observe and understand that the hand of the Lord has done this, the Holy One of Israel has created it" (Is 41:20). "Not your hand, not your personhood, not you, but My hand, the Holy One of Israel has done this." It's amazing. This is what He's talking about—you just be little. You just be humble. You stand in truth of who you truly are and let Me be the God here. You will have no other god before Me." And the only other god we try to put before Him is the little god of ourselves, isn't it? It's a beautiful reading.

One of the greatest of all the virtues is humility. Humility is based on Jesus. Humility is total dependence on God and is based on truth. Humility knows and accepts limitations. Humility knows it's a child. Humility knows that it's weak. Humility knows it can do nothing without Jesus.

Several years ago I was struggling with this and was asking the Lord, "Why can't we do this? Why can't we do that?" It began to become clear to me because He was starting to enlighten my mind, how very limited we are. We shouldn't be struggling and squirming because we can't do these things, but we should accept our limitations. Accepting our weaknesses is the very act that makes God come into us in greater strength and power. That is when I began to realize, "Lord, You deliberately made us limited." I'll never forget the day I got that light. He was smiling. Have you ever kind of just sensed someone smiling like, "Yes, you got it." I said, "You made us this way so that we will always need You. You never, ever intended us to do one single thing without You."

We are limited in every aspect of our lives, but God is not, and so when we reach our limitations, we have to go over into lack of limitations. When we reach our limit of patience, we just draw on His. When we reach our limit of "I just can't love anymore, I can't be nice anymore, I can't even smile anymore," we go over into His because He said, "I'm not limited. It's yours for the asking." He doesn't want to be left out of anything we do. He made us limited so we would need Him. He wants to be needed. Humility will let us know that we need Him.

Humility is tremendously enfleshed on Calvary, yet we still like to look at the Babe of Bethlehem. It's so awesome that a God so great, so big, a Creator of the whole world, the Second Person of the Trinity who is part of all creation could not only come into us as flesh but as that tiny, helpless baby. This is why, in humility, we can everyday go and adore Him, as we sing at Christmas, "Oh come, let us adore Him."

Two of the main fruits of humility are truth and obedience. We can't really tell for sure if we're humble. If a person says, "I'm think I'm really growing in humility," be careful. But if a person is saying, "I'm growing more docile to the Spirit; I'm growing more submissive to God; I'm growing more in acceptance of His will for me, His plan, His way," then that person is truly growing in humility. When Our Lady said to the servants at Cana (and we are all servants and handmaids of the Lord), "Do whatever He tells you" (Jn 2:5), she is giving us the key to humility: obedience. Humility can only be recognized by its fruit, and its main fruit will be obedience.

Humility gives us tremendous power in intercession. In the epistle to the Hebrews, we read, "He was heard because of His reverence" (Heb 5:7). Humility will always be reverent because humility knows that God is God, and I am not. Humility knows that God is the Father, and I am but the child. Humility has a right order. Scripture says, "God resists the proud (who would ever want to be resisted by God?) but bestows his favor on the lowly" (Jas 4:6). It's interesting that the authority of prayer warriors comes from humility.

Another fruit of humility is gratitude. Are we grateful? Are we grateful for all the little things that people do for us all day long? Are we grateful for all the little and big things that God does for us all day long? As we become aware of how much we have to be grateful for, we become aware of our littleness and our

81

poverty and God's greatness and His generosity and His giftedness. Our focus starts to change. Humility is a wonderful sign that we are making progress.

Humility is truth. That's why if we say, "Oh, I'll never do that again," that's not really truth. How do we know? We hope we'll not do something again, or we hope we won't say something again, but that depends on God's grace in our walk with Him. The way of the child is incredibly important because the Spirit will counsel us constantly on what to do and what to say, or not to say, if we but stop and check it out and ask. That's humility. Catherine Doherty of Madonna House in Canada often prayed, "Oh Lord, give me the heart of a child and the courage to follow it." This truly is a prayer for all prayer warriors.

Take a moment to quiet yourself
and rest your head upon Jesus' heart.
Become aware of His tremendous love for you.
Allow His love to fill you as you are drawn
into the Lord's ocean of mercy and love.
Then prayerfully consider the following questions.

EXAMINATION OF CONSCIENCE—PRIDE

Daily life

Where do I think too highly of myself?

Where do I willingly choose and claim as my own what belongs to God?

Where do I have an excessive love of self in my thoughts? in my words? in my actions?

How is this reflected in the way I dress? the car I drive? my house? my possessions?

How is this excessive love of self reflected in the way I spend my money, time, and talent?

In what ways do I still serve two masters?

Where is my sin of pride acting as the gateway to other sins, especially spiritual sloth, envy, and anger?

Pride of Intellect

In what ways am I attached to my judgment and thoughts, with the emphasis on natural knowledge that I have attained myself?

Am I unwilling to listen to another's position and discernment?

Do I often find myself thinking, "I already know that" when someone is giving me counsel or advice?

In what situations am I unwilling to be open and learn, especially from God?

Where is my pride killing my faith?

Where am I so "full" of my own knowledge that I am not open to having my soul filled with God's light in prayer?

Where is my intellect an obstacle to contemplation and union with God?

Where do I have a tendency to presume too greatly on my own abilities and gifts?

Do I feel that I am so far advanced spiritually that I do not need a spiritual director to guide and direct me?

Am I a perfectionist?

Pride of Authority / Superiority

Where is my excessive self-love leading me to be domineering, overbearing, arrogant, critical, argumentative, bossy, and offensive?

What is my attitude toward those in authority over me?

Do I willingly welcome their advice, encouragement, and correction, or am I rigid and unbending? Do I think that it has to be my way, or I'm not doing it?

Do I treat those in authority in a reverent way?

Do I have difficulty accepting God and His Church as my authority?

Where are my actions saying "My will be done" rather than "Thy will be done"?

Do I desire God's counsel?

Do I willingly obey whatever He tells me?

In what situations do I want to control the lives of others?

Where does my sin of pride readily lead me into angry feelings, words, thoughts, and actions?

Do I have a tendency to think that I am better than others?

Where am I apathetic to the rights and feelings of others?

Pride of Ambition

Do I crave praise, recognition, and places of honor?

Does my ambition to be #1 cause me to dominate those "beneath me"?

Am I overly competitive, seeking places of honor that others hold?

Do I impose my own ideas and ways of doing things on others?

Where am I bossy, demanding my own way?

Where do I exert my influence in order to get my own way?

What am I doing to correct my overbearing, critical attitude?

In what situations do I have a tendency to think that I am better than others are?

Pride of Timidity

Do I have a timid disposition?

If so, has my timidity become a habit and been carried to the extreme that I avoid doing what I should do or do what I should not do?

Has my timidity become a strong habit leading to a lack of
self-confidence, fear of ridicule, and little courage and
strength to keep resolutions?
Has my habit of timidity caused me to lose hope because I
believe my weaknesses are too strong?
Where do I use my timidity to hide my weaknesses and imper-
fections for fear of ridicule?
How do I view my weaknesses?
Do I overexaggerate my weaknesses?
Do I avoid doing things because I might not be the best?
Do I use my weakness as an excuse because of fear of failure?
In what situations does my fear of failure limit God's ability to
use me?
Where am I allowing my fear of ridicule to hold me back on my
spiritual journey?

Pride of Sensitiveness

Do my feelings get wounded and hurt easily?
In which situations do I most easily feel offended?
Which persons do I most readily take offense from?
Do I feel unloved and unwanted, thinking that others are
purposely trying to hurt me?
Am I easily wounded with every lack of recognition or
supposed neglect?
Am I a forgiving person?
Do I forgive others right away, or do I hold and nurse a grudge
and prevent reconciliation?
Do I receive a false joy out of feeling badly over these
perceived hurts?
Do I speak coldly to or refuse to speak to those who have hurt
me?
In what situations have I made it a habit to cling to previous
hurts?
Do I experience self-satisfaction and self-righteousness in not
being on speaking terms with another?
Can I laugh at my mistakes? Can I laugh with others about my
mistakes?
Do I resent corrections, advice, help, or favors?
Does my pride of sensitivity prevent unity in my family and
community?

Does my pride of sensitivity force others to have to "walk on eggshells" so as to not hurt my feelings?

Pride of Complacency (Vanity)
Is the opinion and esteem of others more important to me than God's opinion and esteem of me?
> Does my craving to be well-thought-of lead me to think, speak, or act in a vain way?
> Do I work hard to uphold my reputation even if that reputation may not be totally truthful?

Where does my vanity displace my focus from living my life to bring honor and glory to God to living to please others?
> Do I misuse my God-given talents hoping to receive the praise and esteem of others?

Am I vain about my personal looks, strength, talents, athletic ability, or possessions?
> Does my sin of vanity cause me to become like the Pharisees, thinking too highly of myself, while looking down on others?
> Has my vanity caused me to become boastful, hypocritical, stubborn, disobedient, and critical?
> Do I have an overbearing, haughty, "holier than thou" attitude?
> Do I carry myself in a conceited, vain way?
> What can I do to be more welcoming in my countenance?

Do I use my gifts or perform any spiritual works, devotions, or outward pious actions in order to be noticed by my spiritual director or others?
> Do I minimize or hide my faults with my spiritual director?
> Do I tend to withhold information from my spiritual director?

Do I seek the esteem and praise of others for my spiritual works?
Is the real motivation behind my spiritual works, devotions, and pious actions to make me feel good?

In my spiritual life
As I progress spiritually has a secret pride developed within me, leading to complacency with myself and my spiritual accomplishments?
> Have I begun to almost condemn others in my thoughts or actions who don't have similar devotions and spirituality?
> Do I find myself witnessing more to myself than to God?

Where do I have trouble being obedient to God's word to me?

Where does my pride cause me to take my focus off God and put it on myself?

In my spiritual journey, where do I take the credit rather than giving God the glory?

Do I desire a higher degree of prayer without going through the necessary stages like everyone else?

How does my excessive love of self prevent me from entering into the purification process more fully?

Do I have a problem with spiritual pride?

Do I flee from and harbor hostility against those who correct me on my spiritual journey?

When do I prefer to instruct rather than to be instructed (when I should be learning)?

Where does spiritual pride in my life turn me away from the contemplation of divine things?

Where is my pride blinding my understanding and leading me into spiritual self-delusion?

Do my occasions of false piety cause others to turn away from wanting to be holy?

****

Embracing humility

How does the way I live my life show that I view my talents and abilities truly as gifts from God?

Which of my talents and abilities do I have a tendency to believe are due to my own efforts?

What am I doing to practice the virtue of humility in situations where I am tempted to think too highly of myself?

Where am I claiming glory for myself rather than directing all praise to the Father?

In what ways is embracing humility difficult for me?

Where am I still attached to my own will? my own good works? others' opinion of me?

What am I doing to develop the spirit of poverty within myself?

Where do I need to become more dependent upon God?

What efforts am I making to embrace humility?

Where is my pride keeping me from knowing God in a more intimate way? from knowing others in a more intimate way?

What can I do to create a more docile, obedient spirit within myself?

87

Ministry

Do I present an attitude of superiority over those with whom I pray in my words, thoughts, or actions?

After successful ministry, do I claim as my own the glory and honor that belongs to the Father?

Am I boastful or full of pride about my spiritual progress, discernment, and prayer power?

When I witness to others, do I tell people about myself, or do I tell them about God?

What can I do to empty my heart of self so that I can hold more of God's people there?

Does my focus on self and my needs cause me to miss being open to pray some of the prayers God would like me to pray throughout the day?

Where does my judgmental opinion of others have a negative effect on the unity of my family and community's prayer?

As you study your responses to the above questions, you may find that you have a tendency towards one or two types of pride. Which type of pride attacks you most? Journal with the Lord about this tendency, asking for His understanding, wisdom, and counsel as you journal. What is it that the Lord would like to reveal to you right now?

In the upcoming week focus on the one area of weakness that seems to be predominant. Make a specific resolution on how you will work to overcome this tendency, incorporating what the Lord has revealed to you in your journaling. Let the Lord pace you. Do not try to do too much in too short a time.

Review your resolutions often. Pray and ask the Lord to fill you with His love, mercy, and forgiveness and a desire to embrace humility.

Chapter 5

Gluttony

When the Lord was calling me out of the cloister, I was questioned, "How will you live?" I said, "I don't know." So I went back to the Lord and asked, "They're asking me this question: 'How are we going to live?' Are we going to beg?" He said, "No." I said, "Are we going to work?" He said, "No, you need to be free to be in ministry and to pray." "Well, how are we going to live?" He said, "I'll provide. I'll provide. I will give you all that you need but not all that you desire." There's quite a difference between what we need and what we desire. I have found out in my journey with the Lord there's really very little that we need, but there's a lot that we desire, and we see this a lot in eating and drinking.

St. Thomas Aquinas defines gluttony as an "inordinate desire in eating and drinking" (*A Tour of the Summa*, 148-4). One of the ways gluttony manifests itself is in taking more than is necessary. The key word here is *necessary*. St. Isidore said, "A gluttonous person is excessive in what, when, how, and how much he/she eats and drinks" (*De Summ. Bon II*). Again, we are talking about excessive: more than is necessary, more than we need. It's interesting to really examine ourselves. Am I taking more than what is necessary? This will make us stop and be more aware of the presence of God and more aware of what we are doing. How many times do we just eat or drink out of habit and aren't even aware until the meal is over, and we say, "Oh, my goodness, I'm just stuffed." Then we realize, "I wasn't even aware of what I was doing." So the gift of awareness is important here if we're going to be aware of what is necessary.

Another way gluttony can manifest itself is eating or drinking when it's the wrong time. It's not meal time, or it might be a time when I'm not even hungry. There's that unredeemed self saying, "I want what I want when I want it." Gluttony can demand perfectly prepared foods. We can see this in restaurants when something was ordered and it isn't prepared exactly the way it was ordered. We can see a tremendous overreaction in people sometimes as anger or rudeness at the waiter or waitress. Watch that. If that comes forth within ourselves, we are into an attachment that can be very demanding.

Gluttony wants expensive foods and wines. It will attach a great deal of importance to the quality of food or wine or drink and will not be satisfied with what is common. Feeling negative about the food placed in front of us or complaining about it are little signs that, "Uh, oh. I'm tapping into this capital sin of gluttony."

Gluttony is more than simply overeating. It is really an abuse of God's gifts. Food is necessary for good health and wholeness, but this sin is an abuse of God's gift to us. In the parable of Lazarus and the rich man, the rich man ate and drank and had his banquet all the time. When he died, he was just parched, begging for food, begging for drink, but he couldn't be reached. He was on the other side. This is a pretty high penalty for someone who was excessive. Lazarus, who was the beggar at that time, now was at the banquet. God looks at this very seriously. So gluttony is not only being excessive in what we eat and drink, but it's not sharing with those who don't have. I think this is what brought this severe judgment on the rich man.

We have to be careful that we stay out of the spirit of the world. We live in a world that puts a great deal of emphasis on food. The world uses the term "diet"; the Church uses the term "fasting." Both have a discipline, but the motives are quite different as a rule. Dieting is usually for myself, while fasting is for God. Our motives make all the difference in the world. So once again, it goes back to a person's motive, their attitude, what they are doing it for or whom they are doing it for. We can see why we can never judge another person—we really don't know. But we need to know ourselves, so we can know what *our* motive is. Am I doing this for God, or am I doing this for myself? Our excessive concern for our bodies can make it a sin of self-love and self-indulgence. Gluttony will lead us to addictions as well. It will lead us to anything so that the emptiness can be filled.

So one of the basic roots of gluttony is an unconscious self-image of emptiness. It may be a conscious image for some, but often it is an unconscious self-image, and we start feeding that emptiness with food. I once read an article entitled, "What's eating you?" If we start overeating or overindulging, usually

90

something is eating at us. It could be loneliness, depression, extreme stress, anxiety, or frustration. There are a lot of ways to be empty. There are a lot of ways to feel empty. As we pray, the Lord will reveal to us these empty areas within us and will show us how we are trying to feed this emptiness.

We live in a culture where a great deal of emphasis is on the body. I think this is a sign of the culture of death that our Holy Father is talking about. It is interesting that when we forget to take care of our spiritual lives and our souls, then somehow we start to take better care of our bodies. We shift the focus more to the physical. When the body starts becoming overly important, usually it is the soul that is suffering. In the United States there are more athletic clubs than retreat houses. We live in a nation that is putting a great deal of emphasis on exercising. Sometimes we have lost the balance of the spiritual exercising, the spiritual exercises that our souls need. We are not saying exercising isn't good, it is, but God want us to be in balance. We need both. We need physical food, but we also need spiritual food.

It's interesting that Jesus began His public ministry by fasting. He had already come out of a life of poverty, simplicity, hiddenness, silence, and solitude. He was extremely disciplined, and yet He began His public life by fasting. We would think He would be well-prepared to go to that wedding at Cana, but He went into the desert on a forty-day fast. So He is trying to show us something of the tremendous tension between the spirit world and the flesh. There's always that dichotomy and struggle. Jesus tells us do not worry about our livelihood, what we are to eat or drink or use for clothing. He tells us life is more than food, and the body is more valuable than clothes. We are not to worry about our life or what we will eat (see Mt 6:25). Well we do, don't we? Sometimes we worry about what we eat or what we don't eat. It's interesting to see where our thoughts really are.

When we fast for two or three days, we will see something happening to our bodies. It will start to release poisons, and we'll start to get energy. We'll start to feel wonderful. We don't quite have that experience in a one-day fast. But in a two- or three-day fast or a fast like Jesus did, our whole bodies will change if we're fasting correctly. Jesus was fasting from food, but He was not fasting from prayer. He was not fasting from God's love. The Lord showed me that what happens physically in the individual body during a fast can happen throughout the whole Mystical Body as well. We can fast (even just a few people), representing the Mystical Body, and as poisons are released from our bodies, we can actually release Satan from the Mystical Body. Fasting has a tremendous mystical power.

I didn't know this for a long time. I knew fasting was good for us, but I didn't know it had a deliverance power until God revealed it to me. "This kind does not leave but by prayer and fasting" (Mk 9:29 RSV). But Satan knows that. I think this is one of the ways he uses gluttony very subtly because he doesn't want us to fast.

Now there is a correct way to fast. When we were in the cloister, we fasted all the time. It was a very austere penitential lifestyle. We didn't think anything about it. It was just a way of life. We fasted every week. It was easy. But when I came home from the cloister, I had a very difficult time fasting. I found myself getting very fatigued. Finally, I asked the Lord, "I can't understand why I'm having a difficult time fasting. I am so tired all the time. I'm getting headaches. What's wrong?" He let me understand, "In the first place, you're not fasting correctly because you're not eating correctly. If you want to fast correctly, you have to eat correctly so that you will have the energies to fast." In the cloister, we ate correctly; we ate things that gave us high energy. But now I was living on my own, and I really didn't pay much attention to what I ate. I would just grab something. If we don't eat properly, we usually will not fast properly either. They go together.

He also let me know that in the convent we all were fasting together. We had an audience, so to speak, but out here on my own, no one knew. No one knew if I was sacrificing this or that, and that made it a little bit more difficult. Fasting cuts right through that subtle self-love. It cuts right through self-centeredness. No one is watching us except God. No one knows that we are fasting, but that makes it pure. It's all for His greater honor and glory. This showed the purity of motive, which I really didn't have, to fast when no one knows we're fasting and to sacrifice when only God knows. We need deeper purification and fasting to purify our motive. So it was a good lesson for me. Fasting has a even greater power when it's done only for God to see and not anyone else, but oftentimes that can make it more difficult.

Several years ago on one of our trips to Medjugorje, I asked Our Lady, "Do you want us to fast on bread and water?" At this time I didn't have the community with me, and I was still living alone. I was eating on the run. She said, "No, I don't want you to fast on bread and water. I want you to fast from fast foods." She's a good mother. She said, "I want you to eat properly, like a few more vegetables." She told me the things that she wanted me to eat. She said, "I want you to have high energy because God has work for you to do." So fasting for me meant I had to plan my meals, prepare them, and eat properly. A discipline had come that wasn't there before, and I felt great.

When we're out on missions, we have to spend a great deal of time preparing the talks because we give one right after another. So around the clock, we're preparing talks in the hotel rooms, and Sr. Jane and I have noticed that we're rarely hungry. We practically forget to eat. We just take some cheese and crackers or something in our suitcase, and we don't even eat anywhere else. I think it's because we're being so fed. Have you ever experienced when you're really in prayer and you're true to your prayer and journaling and you're being fed, gluttony really isn't a problem, is it? There is a tremendous moderation and balance that comes. We need both kinds of food, but prayer is one of the great antidotes for this particular capital sin of gluttony.

We need to cultivate this spiritual hunger and thirst if we do not have it. Why don't I have a hunger and thirst for prayer or for Mass or for Scripture? Why don't I have a hunger and thirst for good solid spiritual reading or to hear about Jesus or to talk about Him?" These are little signs that can tell us if we are spiritually well.

We have sheep at home and they love to eat, but they need to be led to the pasture. They need to be fed. Sheep are quite helpless really. They need the shepherd. God knows that we are the same. We are the sheep of His green pasture. He knows we need to be fed. Jesus told us to labor not for food that perishes, but for food that remains (see Jn 6:27). Jesus is the Bread of Life. It is like Jesus is saying to us, "I will feed you with Myself, not only at Mass, not only in the Eucharist, but I'll feed you every day in prayer and we'll cast out this gluttony."

Satan tempts us through food. It's very interesting that the first sin in the Garden had to do with food. Eve was tempted. Scripture says, "The woman saw that the tree was good for food, pleasing to the eyes, and desirable for gaining wisdom" (Gn 3:6). The temptation worked. It was a powerful temptation. Satan tried it again with Jesus. Jesus was led by the Holy Spirit into the desert after having fasted for forty days. Jesus was hungry by now. Temptations come, by the way, when we're hungry, when we are empty, and are feeling empty. That's when temptations come, and so the temptation came, "If You are the Son of God, command these stones to turn into bread" (Mt 4:3). The temptation came through food, and Jesus did not fall. Jesus said, "Doing the will of Him who sent Me and bringing His work to completion is My food" (Jn 4:34).

What Gluttony Looks Like in Me

One of the ways I can tell very simply at our table if someone is more interested in food than in anything else is that nothing gets passed. The food gets passed to them, then they put it on their plate and start eating because their interest is more in the food. Or have you ever seen someone start to eat, and it looks like they are attacking their food? It harms charity because if that becomes our primary focus, then we're not interested in conversation. We had somebody in our community one time who just sat and ate and ate, and when he was through eating, then he would talk. He said, "This is the way I was raised. We sat at the table, ate, and then talked." I said, "Well, that's not what we do here." Charity comes first; eating is second. Eating is a social thing.

In my earlier days, I was very forceful when I wanted to do a particular fast. One Lent I wanted to do a very extreme severe fast only on fruit juice. My spiritual director was not in favor of it, but I had some friends who were doing it, and it just sounded like a real saintly, extraordinary thing to do. So I begged him and told him a million reasons why I should do this fast. I said, "Well, I'd really like to try it. It's Lent and my friends are doing it." He understood that new converts have a lot of zeal. We kind of run outside the racetrack half the time, but he didn't want to pull me in too tightly, so he said, "All right, but we'll watch it very closely and see how you do." I had his okay, but really I was forcing him.

It was a very difficult week. I got stomach pains, felt horrible hunger, and could hardly work at my job or at my Legion of

Mary work. I was irritable and extremely tired. I just couldn't wait for the week to be over. It was kind of a "grin and bear it" thing. "I'm going to stick to this because I'm committed to it." But it was not humility. It really wasn't a service to the Lord at all. He didn't want it, but God let me go through it to teach me a very important lesson about fasting.

At the end of the week, I was in prayer thanking God that it was over, and He gave me an image of an apple. He said, "What do you think of this apple?" I said, "It's beautiful. It's highly polished." It just started turning very slowly, and when it got around to the other side there was this horrible looking little worm coming out of it. He said, "You see that worm? Do you know what that worm is?" I said, "It's me, isn't it? It's my pride. We can ruin anything You want to do if we want to have it our way." Even fasting can be self-centered and full of self-love. It can get us all puffed up for our own honor and glory, "Look at me." I made it through the week, but it wasn't pleasing to God at all. So we have to be careful that our fasting is regulated by obedience and by what God wants.

We see gluttony in many different addictions today. Every addiction will tap into the Seven Capital Sins. We're seeing tremendous misuse of the earth and resources that God has given to us, which is another form of gluttony.

Bottom line, gluttony is going to be attachment to my present life. It's that need that I have right now, for whatever reason; it's going to feed me. Jesus said, "Reform your lives" (Mt 4:17). Today I hear it as I've never heard it before. I heard it as, "Reshape your life. Change things. You have to do it." I heard Him say, "Use your own free will. You need to make some choices." I heard Him say it to me personally, and I heard Him say it to our whole community. "Reform your lives." We have to make some changes now.

In My Spiritual Life

Spiritual gluttony is something we can be guilty of day after day without even realizing it. It is loving God more for what He can give us (consolations and experiences) than for Himself. We especially find this in beginners, in newly baptized converts, and in people newly baptized in the Holy Spirit.

Beginners have a tendency to go into prayer for what they can get out of it. It the early stages of the spiritual life, we can be much more interested in what we are going to get than Who is giving it to us. It is easy to do this because God baits us with consolations, and so we get used to the consolations because that's what our prayer is. Consolations are God's gifts, and just like a little child, we can become more interested in what we are going to receive than what we're going to give. It becomes more about the consolations and experiences than about God. It's about what we are going to receive. It's a mentality of keeping it all to ourselves. If we stay here and don't move on to deeper spiritual maturity, then we can move into spiritual gluttony.

This is exactly what Satan wants. He can enter into our spiritual lives when he sees we're always seeking that spiritual high, that experience, or God doing something for me. Satan is watching for that because he knows that we won't grow if he can keep us here spiritually. If he can introduce spiritual gluttony into our lives, he will keep us here so that we won't grow in faith or belief that God is with me and loves me. So we have to be careful.

We have seen this pattern now in the other Capital Sins, also: Satan attacks the flesh. He can't attack God directly, but he will attack God in our flesh if he can because the flesh is weak. Jesus said, "The spirit is willing, but the flesh is weak" (Mt 26:41; Mk 14:38). Satan hates flesh, he hates the whole Incarnation, and so he attacks the flesh. He will encourage us to seek spiritual highs because it sounds good—it's spiritual. It may be wonderful to want these experiences and consolations, but really it's deadly.

As a new convert, I read the lives of the saints, and I remember reading the life of St. Germaine. She would be peeling the potatoes and would start sailing right up in the kitchen. I thought, "Oh, that'd be great. It would be wonderful to have the gift of levitation. I wonder what it would be like to have a relationship with God like that." If we are unconsciously seeking the experience, Satan can enter and take us right off the pathway of obedience and the honest-to-God perfection of being filled with God's love. It will take us out of humility and purity of motivation. It is very clever how he can use something that looks good and make it so harmful. Satan likes those spiritual highs, and unfortunately, there are many false mystics in the world today that live out of that.

Spiritual gluttony has fruits of selfishness and self-centeredness. It is focused on what I can get out of this prayer experience and what I'm going to get out of the relationship. This can happen even at Communion. We can be more interested in what the Lord is going to say to us, or how we're going to feel, or what grace we're going to receive, rather than being focused on, "This is God. This is the Gift Himself." When God begins to see us going this way, then the Spirit will lead us into one of the dark nights of the soul and spirit for our own good, to strip us of the excess, our "gimme, gimme" complex, so we can grow in maturity. God can take away the consolations in a second. All of a sudden, we will have a distaste for something we really enjoyed spiritually. We fight the dark night because it will start to strip us of all self-satisfaction that we've been living on. It's hard to switch gears. This is where a spiritual director can help us walk the walk because in the dark night we can't see. It's dark. There is no one to look at. We can't even see Jesus, but when we're in the dark with someone we love, we know they're there. There's a presence.

So we begin to intuit at a deeper level. It's a deeper faith walk. We begin to change our focus because we are leaning more on Him and what He is saying. Now we go more on what we hear Him saying than on what we are seeing. It's a different way of knowing. It's a faith walk. So it is a beautiful thing when the Holy Spirit starts stripping us of the unhealthy things that were feeding us. This can be God, stripping us of all the exterior so we will grow into a deeper relationship with Him—not for what He can do for us, but for who He is to us. Once we start to make the passover into deeper spiritual maturity, the love of self will start to fade away, and we will begin to focus more on God's love.

Spiritual gluttony can harm us physically, mentally, and spiritually—body, soul, and spirit—because ultimately it's shutting out God. Spiritual dullness and sluggishness can come, tapping into the capital sin of sloth. Spiritual gluttony will eventually kill any fervor that we have or desire for spiritual things because ultimately we're focusing on ourselves and are slipping into the world. It's a very childish level of prayer that is strictly for beginners. We don't want to stay there because in the spiritual life, we either move ahead or regress. We can't stay too long in any one place. We would regress if we stayed with spiritual gluttony to the point where we lost all appetite for prayer and spiritual things. Eventually, it will lead to a total inability to pray. The main problem is that I am focusing on *my* needs and no one else's. This is why intercession has such tremendous power; it does not focus on me. If it does focus on me, then it's not intercession.

One of the fruits that Satan is after in spiritual gluttony is to have us start telling our spiritual directors with finality what God is doing and what God is saying. In these instances, directees end up directing their directors, particularly if their spiritual directors don't have a strong gift of discernment and only see all these wonderful things going on in a person's life. A spiritual director can begin to believe everything the directee is saying and not discern which spirits are moving there. We always have to go back and ask ourselves: am I obeying my spiritual director or those who have authority over me? Is there purity in my life and in my motives? Am I truly striving for perfection, for holiness, to really be full of God's love?

Obedience is a good criteria for us to know if we are falling into spiritual gluttony. To know if the mystical experiences that we are having are authentic, we can look at whether or not we are little and humble and manifesting that through obedience. If so, our experiences probably are authentic. But if these mystical experiences start to take over because "God said" or "I'm understanding this" or "experiencing that" and obedience kind of goes out the window, particularly to those we are accountable to, it would be very questionable if it is the Lord.

This kind of false mysticism will lead us to judge others and put them down. "How come you're not going to Mass everyday? How come you're not fasting more?" A spiritual director can pick up right away that there's uncharitableness coming through here. Obviously some of these experiences that might have started out as God and with God, now are not God. The enemy has taken over and spiritual gluttony has set in.

If there is spiritual pride coupled with spiritual gluttony, it will lead us into false mysticism very quickly because we will be seeking one spiritual experience after another. Many false mystics go down the slippery slope of spiritual gluttony because it leads to seeking oneself more in prayer than in seeking God. We have to be careful in our prayer lives that we're not seeking the spiritual experience, but we're seeking God. If God wants to give us an experience of Himself, fine, but we have to be careful not to just seek the experience. Often the experience will come when we least expect it.

Another way to spot whether or not gluttony is activated in our lives is if we have a great aversion to sacrifice, suffering, and the Cross. We have no desire to lay down our lives, and we can turn more and more into ourselves. We have no desire to do anything for anyone. Spiritual gluttony will show up particularly as a lack of desire to intercede, as intercession is strictly for others. We can lose interest very quickly because there's nothing in it for me.

Another checkpoint to watch for is self-imposed penance, particularly fasting, if it has not approved by our spiritual director. It can be very dangerous. We need to be careful if we are doing something and concealing it from our spiritual director or if we are rather forceful in convincing our spiritual director that we should do a particular penance or fast.

Spiritual Warfare

There are quite a few evil spirits that move in families and clusters that are associated with gluttony. There is a spirit of infirmity where we think someone is ill, but they really are not. It usually comes in through this spirit of gluttony or the spirit of retaliation. There are spirits of nonsense, games, and trivia. A spirit of confusion will show up here. There is also a spirit of rejection, which will often be the controlling spirit because whatever we are experiencing is a form of not being loved in some way. If we are experiencing some kind of alienation or rejection and are not being filled up by God in daily prayer, not looking at these things within us, Satan can come right into our house and take up residency through this spirit of rejection.

This is why self-knowledge is so important. Satan hates God. That's a hard concept for some of us to understand: he hates God, but he can't strike directly at God. He's been banished, but he can still try to strike at God within us, in these temples. He strikes at the flesh because he's trying to strike at God. He hates the Incarnation and Incarnational spirituality. The more he can strike at our flesh, then indirectly he is striking at God.

Paul says, "Draw your strength from the Lord and His mighty power" (Eph 6:10). We draw our strength from the Lord because there's a tremendous battle in this sin area. We need this part of the armor to stand firm and draw our strength from the Lord.

Remedies

Gift of the Holy Spirit: Fortitude

The beautiful gift of Fortitude is a gift of courage to "hang in there" no matter what. You may have heard the story of a person who was climbing a mountain. He fell over and grabbed a hold of a twig that was hanging out there. He was hanging on for dear life calling, "Help, help, help!" Pretty soon God answered. "Oh God, Oh God. Thank You. You're there." "I'm here." "Oh God, help me! What should I do? What should I do?" And the Lord said, "Let go." This person climbing the mountain said, "Is there anybody else up there?"

Sometimes we keep thinking, "Oh God, Oh God. I don't have the courage." And then He'll say, "Let go. Let go." This is the gift of Fortitude. It will take over. "You will have My courage. You will have My strength. It's going to be okay. It's going to give you the strength to suffer. Fortitude will give you the strength for mortification, for self-denial, for fasting. It's going to remove that terrible fear of the Cross. But let go." It's hard to let go because there's an emptiness within us if we're not in prayer, and so we want to feed ourselves.

This gift of Fortitude will start to powerfully root out the sin of gluttony within us. There is a lot of fear in putting oneself to death. There's a lot of fear of sacrifice, suffering, and the Cross. The gift of Fortitude will take away this fear of suffering. It gives us tremendous strength. The Spirit will direct us toward whatever God wants. The gift of Counsel will direct us, but it is the gift of Fortitude that's going to strengthen us to do whatever Counsel tells us and give us courage to take that next step.

The gift of Fortitude is extremely helpful as we put our wants and desires to death. We need courage to do that. It takes courage to die daily to our wants and desires. Then we will know that we are free from this area because there will be no attachment. The Lord said in the Song of Songs, "Come, my friends." He calls us friends. "Come, My friends, and drink deeply of love. Drink deeply of love" (see Sng 5:1). "Come, you who are hungry or thirsty and I will satisfy you. If you are hungry and thirsting for holiness, for Me, you will be satisfied." He's trying to set us on the right path of what we should be hungering and thirsting for. The gift of Fortitude gives us the courage to seek the higher way. Jesus always wants to provide for our needs. In prayer, we can cast out the spirit of gluttony because in prayer God will feed us, He will nurture us, and He will satisfy us as He promised.

Words from the Cross

We have to keep coming back to Jesus' fifth word from the Cross, "I thirst" (Jn 19:28). He had to have been physically thirsty as He had lost a lot of blood, but He was thirsting for love also. It's a double thirst. He has us go through that same kind of thirst so that we can repair this sin of excessive love of self and the flesh. When we thirst, particularly if we're thirsting for love or union with God, for His word or any revelation from Him, for His presence, for any intervention of God in our lives, then we are healthy.

I remember reading about one of the Desert Fathers. Someone went out to the desert to ask him, "Teach me how to pray." The desert father took him to a little oasis, they waded into it, and he dunked this person's head down almost like he was baptizing him, but he didn't let him come right back up. He just held his head under that water and pretty soon, this man came up gasping and upset. "I can hardly breathe." And the desert father said, "When you want God as much as you just wanted that air, then that's how to pray." When we can hunger and thirst like that for God, then we are very healthy.

Before I entered the convent, I was in the Legion of Mary and was praying with a nun who was dying, or so they thought. It was beautiful to meet her and to pray with her. When I asked her how I could pray for her, she said, "Pray that I get an appetite. If I get an appetite, then I know my body will start to heal, and I'll be on my way." That's true. If the body is hungry, that's a good sign it's alive. At her convent they were practically preparing her funeral. In fact, her blood sister, who was also in the convent, had already taken her good Sunday habit and shoes because she knew her sister wasn't going to come home alive from the hospital, and she could especially use the extra shoes.

Well, lo and behold, God gave her an appetite, and both of those sisters are still living today. They must be in their eighties or nineties. But this really impressed me: when we are spiritually hungry or spiritually thirsty, it's a sign of health. We can rest on that. Sometimes we think, "Is there something wrong with me? I'm so hungry for the Lord. I'm so thirsty for His touch, for His love." This is a sign that spiritually we're alive and really quite well. So, "I thirst," isn't all that bad. It's a good sign that we're spiritually alive and need that food and drink that only God can give us.

Once I had a dream of all these people roaming around in a desert, looking for something. I could tell they were hungry. I went up to a man dressed like a monk (who I discerned later was Jesus) and said, "What is it they're looking for?" He said, "The Jesus Spring. The Living Water." There is a hunger and a thirst in God's people. We are looking for the Living Water. This fifth word of the Cross is really important for us, not only to uproot the sin of gluttony within ourselves, but to help other people get out of the flesh and receive the grace of a spiritual hunger.

I'll never forget my very first Lent in the Catholic Church because during Holy Week everything was focused on the Cross. As a convert this was very new to me. I wasn't used to seeing a body on a Cross, and so I was just mesmerized by Holy Week and the Passion of Jesus. On Good Friday I was meditating on the last words of Jesus, and when it came to this the fifth word, Jesus communicated to me from the Cross. Deep in my soul I heard, "I thirst." I heard it and knew, I just knew, my heart knew: He's thirsting for love, He's thirsting for souls. This is the thirst that He shares with us. This thirst is what sets us into action with zeal because we want to do everything we can, particularly as intercessors, to quench that thirst. If we thirst, we're thirsting for love, but in our thirst for love, we can hopefully quench other people's thirst for love at the same time because they are roaming around. It's like the world is kind of a desert right now, and they're looking for that Living Water, the Jesus-Spring. They're looking for love.

It's really awesome that Jesus, who is the Living Water Himself, thirsts. What He is saying and what He has undergone is tremendous. The paradox is that here is God, who is the Living

Water; here is Jesus who had previously told the woman at the well that He would give her water so that she would never thirst; here is the same Person who changed water into wine; and here *He* is crying out, "I thirst." He is hanging on the Cross in reparation for sin. He is repairing the sin of gluttony. It's really a cry from the heart.

Virtues:
Temperance, Prudence

Temperance is an important virtue as it controls and moderates. We want to eat and drink moderately with discipline. The fruit of temperance will be self-control. Prudence is another important virtue because it gives us the knowledge of how to act. St. Augustine said prudence is "the knowledge of what to seek and what to avoid." It gives us the knowledge. It makes right reason come into action, and it guides the other virtues by setting rules.

St. Paul struggled with this when he said, "I do the things I do not want to do and the things I do not want to do, I do" (Rom 7:15). This beautiful virtue of prudence will give us the knowledge of what to do. One fruit from prudence will be inner strength.

Everything that has to do with fasting or anything that would be excessive should be done under spiritual direction. We have to always seek God's mind, and of course our spiritual director's mind, on what type of fasting and mortification we should be doing. There are so many little ways to put self to death through mortification, which won't harm our health at all.

Practicing mortification is a tremendous remedy to gluttony because it brings our senses under control. It is mostly through the senses that we get attacked in this particular sin area. Mortification brings our eyes under control so we're not looking at things we shouldn't be looking at, and it regulates what we're hearing. It keeps our tongue in check even. What we taste can be mortified literally through fasting. The psalmist said, "Taste and see how good the Lord is" (Ps 34:9). So we go right back to that experience of God in prayer.

When we practice mortification to mortify our senses, the saints tell us to do this in very small ways that are hidden, which will cut through our self-love very quickly. For example, we live in community, and so we can't say, "I don't want this" or "I don't want that." Community means we're living a common life, but there are lots of ways to practice mortification in community. We can take smaller portions. Who is going to know if we take one scoop of mashed potatoes or two? Who is going to know if we would really like to have three scoops but only take one? It's hidden. We're not injuring our health. It's balanced. I knew a very holy priest, and I used to watch him in his little ways of mortification, constantly controlling this area of sin. He would take a piece of bread and some butter, and I watched him butter it. He would break the bread in half, but he never buttered the other half. I never really knew—did he really want that butter on there or didn't he? But God knew.

We can take only one piece of candy even when it's being passed around two or three times, or we can take more. No one really knows. There are so many hidden ways of disciplining our will and putting to death what our senses are craving through mortification. We know, "This is for the Lord. I don't need it. It's not necessary." We have to keep coming back to that. So if there were ever two weapons needed in fighting gluttony, they are self-control and inner-strength.

Additional Helps

One practical remedy to help us counteract gluttony is daily prayer. There is nothing as powerful as daily prayer because that's where we really get fed. He's the Shepherd, and He loves to feed us.

He gave me a little insight just the other day in the Gospel about the feeding of the five thousand with the loaves. They were out of food, and the Apostles said, "It's getting late. These people are hungry. There's nothing to eat." And Jesus said, "Well, you feed them." I never noticed their reaction before. "Well that would take two hundred days of our wages" (see Jn 6:7). They're thinking just of themselves and what they would have to give up. I thought, "That's a lot of wages—two-hundred days. There are only three hundred sixty-five days in a year. That's a lot of their wages." And they went right to that natural plane, "How are we going to feed all these people? We can't do that. That would take all of our money and our own resources."

Then Jesus said, "Have them recline." They sat down in small groups on the green grass. I never heard that before—that they sat down on green grass. It took me right back to the Twenty-third Psalm where He leads the sheep, us, to verdant pastures. He said, "I am the Shepherd. I lead My sheep to verdant pastures. I'll always lead them to green pastures where they can be fed, not to dry, burnt-out grass." I thought, "Lord, You went out to that particular spot. You knew these people would follow You out there to the green grass. You knew You were going to do that miracle and feed them." This is what He does to us in prayer. He's there where the grass is green, and we come to Him in prayer and get fed. He'll feed us all we want. He'll nurture us all we want. This is what happens in daily prayer. This is a tremendous antidote for gluttony because we won't feel that emptiness.

Journaling is a tremendous remedy to help us counteract gluttony because that's where we connect. This is where we receive, right there in black and white, what we need to hear and what we need to know. We can try to get in touch with our frustrations and emptiness and journal it out. Otherwise, we will try to feed ourselves with other things. But in journaling, we can bring that into the light before the Lord.

In the Garden of Olives where Jesus underwent such a passion and struggle in the shedding of His blood because of what He was seeing, He gave His fiat, "Not My will, but Yours be done" (Lk 22:42). Jesus returned to this same mountain for His Ascension. It is very interesting that often our deepest struggles, when it costs us our very life to give that "Yes, Lord," is where we ascend and are set free.

In our struggles, we undergo the Garden of Mount Olivet with Jesus. It's a struggle to discipline ourselves. It's a struggle to put ourselves to death. It would be much easier if God would just do it, but He's trying to strengthen our will. It's a struggle because we're also struggling with the enemy who is always enticing us, "Oh, it's just one little piece. You can start tomorrow." That's the enemy. So a good way to discipline ourselves is to try to simply eat and drink in God's presence. We can imagine that He is at that table with us. He is always with us. It is helpful to be aware that we are constantly in God's presence and have His help at all times.

God wants us to root out gluttony. He wants to call us out of the fleshpots of Egypt. Coming against gluttony is always going to come against self: self-satisfaction, self-glorification, and self-love. It's so subtle in us, isn't it? Self keeps coming up in all these areas of sin.

One Lent in the cloister, I asked the Lord, "How do You want me to fast?" That might seem a silly question because as a cloistered nun I was fasting all the time. And yet, that was what the Spirit was putting on my heart to ask. The Lord led me to Isaiah 58:6-7, "This, rather, is the fasting that I wish: releasing those bound unjustly, untying the thongs of the yoke; setting free the oppressed, breaking every yoke; sharing your bread with the hungry, sheltering the oppressed and the homeless; clothing the naked when you see them, and not turning your back on your own." He said, "I'm glad you asked. This is the kind of fasting I want." I saw how wise God was to give us something positive to do to come against gluttony.

He began to show me where my sin of gluttony was at that particular time in my life. Time was the most precious commodity I had as a cloistered nun. I did a lot of things for the other sisters. We worked very hard at manual labor, and my only bit of free time was on Saturday. The Lord showed me that I was hoarding my free time. I had a gluttonous attitude regarding my free time, "This is mine." Saturday was our time to clean our rooms. I would hurry and clean my room. Housekeeping isn't one of my main gifts, so I just kind of brushed things under the rug. This way I would have more time to myself and could do things that I like to do. I never saw that I was hoarding my time until He gave me that light.

So I said, "Well, what is it You want me to do with this precious time?" He said, "I want you to give it away and do something for someone else. It would be nice if after you clean your room, you would clean an older sister's room as well." There was a pause. "Then it would be nice if you would shine their shoes and get their habits all nice for Sunday Mass." Sunday's a big day in the convent. The sisters dressed in their Sunday best, especially the older sisters, and so that's what I did that Lent. I spent my free time cleaning two older sisters' rooms and shining their shoes and pressing their Sunday habits so they were spick-and-span and beautiful for the Lord on Sunday. They were in seventh heaven! It was a wonderful Lent for me. It was a whole new way to come against things that I was hoarding to myself in a gluttonous fashion, although it had nothing to do with food.

After the Resurrection the Apostles were out in their boats, and Jesus appeared on the shore. He said, "Have you caught anything to eat?" (Jn 21:5) They weren't doing so well without Jesus in the boat, and He was concerned about it. They said, "No." What does Jesus do? He tells them, "Cast your nets on the right side" (Jn 21:6). That's where the fish were. He will tell us how to get food if we go to Him every day. He knows the different ways we need to be fed. He not only will tell us where the food is, but He will provide it for us as He provided it for them. And even better than that, He prepared the food so they could really enjoy it with Him and have a meal together. He will bring us into union, so man and God together can sit down and feast. That's the beauty of prayer. The antidote to gluttony is to allow God to feed us.

Fasting and Feasting

We can *fast from judging others and feast on Jesus in them*. Isn't that beautiful? This gives us something positive to do. Many people find it hard to fast from judging others. Some actually feed on judging others. It feeds their superiority, it feeds their pride, and it feeds their own self-image. We need to take time to look at how do we feed ourselves? This is where this sin comes in - how do we feed ourselves instead of letting God feed us? Jesus told us we have to change and become as little children (see Mt 18:4; Mk 9:35-37) "with a little child to guide them" (Is 11:6). A child can't feed himself; he has to be fed. This is what God is talking about, "Let Me feed you. Quit trying to feed yourself." This is where we are going to start to uproot this sin of gluttony.

We can *fast from words that pollute and feast on phrases that purify*. Have you ever said something out of habit, and it leaves a bad taste in your mouth? "Why did I say that? It didn't give life to anybody. It didn't even make me feel good. Why did I feed myself with that?" These are the roots that we are after. "Why did I have to do that? Why do I have to talk that way? What's in me that is making me think these things?" It's our thoughts that mold us. It's our heart thoughts that mold us. One superior used to say when she was trying to form us, "I can't hear a word you're saying. Your actions are shouting."

We can *fast from discontent and feast on gratitude.* I know people whose whole lifestyle almost is to feed on negativity and criticism: "This could be better. They could have done it better." Or to feed on something about someone else: "Did you see her? Did you see what they're wearing?" Negativity and criticism can become a habit and can feed something within us. So the antidote here would be to feast on gratitude. It's very healing. I can be very discontent with the weather, or we can be very grateful that we even woke up this morning, and God gave us another day.

We can *fast from anger and feast on patience.* Some people live out a lifestyle of anger unconsciously. They're always angry. It feeds them and gives them energy. It's very "safe" because as long as I'm angry, you're not really going to get too close to me, and so you won't hurt me. It's a safeguard to keep people at a distance.

We can *fast from worry and fear and feast on God's providence.* Look at how many times Jesus said, "Do not fear," but we keep on fearing and worrying. We keep being anxious. It's totally against Scripture, and it's feeding something within me. We are looking for the root: why do I do that? Why am I going against this Word of God? This is all tapping into gluttony.

We can *fast from complaining and feast on appreciation.* We can *fast from being negative and feast on affirming.* Affirm others. Affirm yourself. Accentuate the positive. Eliminate the negative. Have you ever been in a conversation where someone give will someone else a compliment, but they'll say, "Yes, but. . . ." It takes you down to hear it, and it takes you down to say it as well.

We can *fast from bitterness and feast on forgiveness.* A lot of people find fasting from bitterness hard because bitterness can be protective. If we're bitter, we don't feel that we have to forgive. We are going to justify ourselves. Our little rationale is going ninety miles an hour. Once bitterness comes, it feeds and feeds and feeds something within me, but once we fast from bitterness, then we can let that go. It's not going to feed us anymore.

We can *fast from self-concern and feast on compassion for others.* We can *fast from discouragement and any kind of knowledge that depresses* (and not let it feed me anymore) *and feast on hope.* When we let depression come in, it robs us. It doesn't feed us; it's not of God. We're going to starve spiritually, emotionally, and physically. It's going to affect relationships. It will distance and separate us.

We can *fast from suspicion and feast on truth.* These are areas where Satan enters and keeps prodding us until we take a suspicion and change it to a fact in our minds. Then we'll move on it, won't we? We can hurt ourselves and hurt others. We need to feast on truth. We can fast from idle gossip and feast on good silence, a pregnant type of silence with God in it.

We can *fast from curiosity and needing to know and feast on trust and faith.* I had a very good friend while I was in the Legion of Mary, who later became a Paraclete priest. I must have been awfully curious at this particular time because I remember he kept saying to me, "Curiosity is not a virtue." It's not a virtue. Curiosity can lead us into a lot of trouble. It has nothing to do with our relationship with the Lord.

We can *fast from thoughts that weaken and feast on promises that inspire*. We can catch these thoughts right away and stop them, "Uh oh. That thought is going to weaken me." If we have self-knowledge, we can stop this process and instead feast on promises that inspire. We can have a wonderful prayer period where God has fed us and has given us promises. But we can take and throw these promises to the four winds as though we never heard God and allow negative thoughts to weaken us and drag us down. This may be what is feeding us instead of God.

All these things have tremendous ripple affects and repercussions. The Spirit will give us different lights and insights so we can go to the very roots of why we do this so we can get it out. This is really what it's about. Who is going to feed whom here? Are we going to try to feed ourselves, or are we going to let God feed us? God is interested in food. He actually chose food as the way to come to us in the Eucharist and to remain with us. Maybe He did that because original sin came out of food. So food is something that's really important, and it can give us life, or it can give us death. This is the paradox of it.

After the Resurrection, the Apostles are fishing and Jesus appeared on the shore as a stranger. He called out, "Have you caught anything yet to eat?" It's amazing the Scriptures where Jesus is interested in food, but it's the food that God wants to give us. Jesus said to His disciples, "I have food that you do not know of. My food is to do the Father's will." When we come into prayer and ask Jesus to feed us and to fill our emptiness, He will. He will nurture us until we are totally satisfied. But we will only be satisfied for a day. He knew that. He taught us to pray, "Give us today, our daily bread" (Mt 6:11). It's daily prayer that will cast out this gluttony, particularly when we are fed with that manna from on High. "Happy are they who have been invited to the wedding feast of the Lamb" (Rv 19:9). He wants us to feast on His grace, on His love, on His presence, on His food.

*Take a moment and quiet yourself
in the presence of the Father.
Rest your heart on His heart
and drink deeply of His love for you.
Pray for a deeper hunger and thirst for the Lord.
Draw your strength from the Lord and His mighty power.*

EXAMINATION OF CONSCIENCE—
GLUTTONY

Personal habits

Do I have an excessive love for food or drink?

Am I excessive in what, when, how, or how much I eat?

  Do I have a tendency to eat any food or drink any beverage in excess?

  Do I experience extreme, but harmful, pleasure from indulging the desires of my flesh?

Do I have a tendency to eat less than what is needed to maintain a healthy body?

  Does my concern or excessive worry about my body-size cause me to be undernourished?

Do I have a tendency to eat more than is necessary to maintain a healthy body?

Am I excessive in what, when, how, or how much I drink?

  Has my drinking recently led to an impairment of right reason?

  Has my eating or drinking led to health problems?

Am I a fussy eater, demanding perfectly prepared or only certain kinds of foods?

  Do I call attention to my likes and dislikes?

Do I feel emptiness deep inside me that I attempt to fill with food, drink, drugs, etc.?

  Do I have a serious problem that needs to be addressed by a professional?

  What is stopping me from seeking help?

In what way does my eating reflect the virtue of temperance? of prudence?

In what way does my drinking reflect the virtue of temperance? of prudence?

Penance and Self-denial

Do I practice self-denial?

    When I fast or do penance am I doing what I want to do or what the Lord has asked me to do?

Do I have the approval of my spiritual director for all my penance, fasting, and mortification?

    Do I add to or change the penance that are approved of by my spiritual director?

    Does the pleasure I experience in my penance cause me to conceal them from my director?

When I practice mortification, do I make it a habit of comparing my offering to that of another person?

    Do I feel a desire to congratulate myself for my penance, fasting, and mortification?

    Do I feel a need to judge or condemn the one with whom I am comparing my offering against?

Do I have a difficult time saying no to pleasure?

Prayer Life

Who or what do I hunger and thirst for?

Do I have an excessive desire to experience consolations and spiritual highs?

    Do I seek consolation more than I seek God?

    Is my heart just as happy to be in desolation as it is to be in consolation?

    Do I act like a spoiled child if each prayer time is not a mountaintop experience?

    Does my seeking spiritual highs tempt me to focus on what I get out of prayer rather than on obedience, spiritual purity, and perfection?

Do I avoid my prayer time, especially my contemplative listening, during times of desolation?

    In times of desolation, how am I cooperating and allowing the Lord to strip away all self-satisfaction so that I can grow in humility and faith?

Has my catering to the desires of my flesh led to spiritual dullness and apathy?

    Do I hurry through my religious duties to get them over with?

Community / Family Life

Do I have a strong aversion and abhorrence of the Cross?

  In what ways do I need to embrace the Cross with *both* hands?

How fervently am I seeking to live the Vows / Promises of the Intercessors of the Lamb of poverty, chastity, obedience, and zeal for souls?

  In what ways can I improve my living out the spirit of the vows?

Do I have a tendency to be selfish?

  Do I focus on my wants and needs, neglecting the needs of my neighbor?

  What do I do to help me remember to think of others first?

Do I indulge the pleasures of my flesh at the expense of my family?

How am I leading my family in the practice of penance?

Consider any areas where you have an openness towards physical and spiritual gluttony. Allow the Holy Spirit to shine His light and show you what He sees. Ask the Lord to show you the reason why you seek consolation in this way, asking for His counsel and guidance. Journal any insights.

Pray for the virtues of temperance and prudence.

Chapter 6

Sloth

The power of prayer warriors is prayer itself. The capital sin of sloth, another head of the dragon, interferes with this power of prayer. St. Thomas defines sloth as "sluggishness of mind which neglects to begin good. It is a kind of oppressive sorrow which so weighs upon a man's mind that he wants to do nothing" (*A Tour of the Summa,* 35-1). It is an inordinate love of rest, which leads us to neglect or omit physical, mental, and spiritual duties. This immediately takes sloth out of the physical realm only and puts it into the mental and spiritual realms as well. There are four major types of sloth: sloth of the intellect, sloth of the will, sloth of the body, and spiritual sloth (which will be discussed later).

Sloth of the intellect is manifested in a sluggishness of thought in useless, vague occupations of the mind. We can be intellectually apathetic, asleep or drowsy, especially at prayer time. Maybe this is why St. Paul says, "It is now the hour for you to wake from your sleep" (Rom 13:11) because there is a sin lurking at the door.

Sloth of the will is when we are really lazy and are not making choices. To not make a choice really is to choose something. Sloth of the will can manifest itself in grumbling or being discontent because everything is not the way we want it to be, so there will be tremendous procrastination. The Spirit will enlighten us to the ways it is manifesting itself in our lives, but basically it's not making the effort. It's a lack of zeal. We might not be making the effort to answer a letter or phone call, particularly to a friend, or putting off the little things like the small chores around the house, or by letting the little things pile up on our desk. Sloth is deceptive because it can be so hidden in these little things. But ultimately, the bottom line of sloth of the will is avoiding obligations and things that we are responsible for and need to be doing.

Sloth of the body is where we have slowed down because of too much ease. We are out of balance. This could be when we're really going at a snail's pace, but this is not the only way it shows itself. Sloth can be extremely deceptive and hidden. One of the main ways we can spot sloth is through busyness. We think of busyness as the total opposite of laziness, but sloth is busyness about the wrong things. It makes us very lazy about the one thing that is necessary. Jesus said to Martha, "Martha, Martha, you are anxious and upset about many things; one thing only is required" (Lk 10:41). We can be busy about many things but neglect our spiritual life and our relationship with God. We might see a person who is very active, doing good things, but they don't have time to pray. They do not have time to journal. They do not have the disciplines of the interior life.

What Sloth Looks Like in Me

We need to take care of ourselves physically, get the proper rest, and eat the right things because if we don't, we can be too physically tired to pray, and sloth can enter in this way. Remember, charity begins at home. We have to take care of ourselves so that we can give our best selves to God.

Sloth is a mental and spiritual laziness that can lead us into a physical laziness. Sloth is very subtle. The spiritual writers tell us that this particular sin is more dominant in our time than in any other. Isn't that interesting? Even with all our gadgets, we don't have enough time to make the effort to grow in our spiritual life. A laziness has set in. It can show up in indifference. "Let someone else do it." It can show up in our not doing something as good as we can. Scripture says, "He (Jesus) has done everything well" (Mk 7:37). Sloth can show up in being half-hearted in our attitude and getting sloppy about something.

As a new convert, all this was brand new to me. I had some habits that the Lord let me see blatantly, especially my first year as a Catholic. I was sharing an apartment with another girl at the time, and my spiritual director called. He was going to come over and bless our pet bird. When he called, he said, "I'll be there in twenty minutes." The apartment was an absolute mess! Housecleaning was not a priority for either of us, so we gathered up the dirty dishes and stuffed them into the oven and swept

115

everything we could into the corners. If there was a rug, we put it under that. That's sloth at its best. It was awful; we only had twenty minutes.

By the time the priest walked in the door the apartment looked rather decent. But later in my prayer, the Lord brought this back to my attention. He began to show me that this is sloth. He said, "That's tremendous irresponsibility. In the first place, I know where the dishes are. I know where the dirt is." He let me understand that it is irresponsible to allow laziness to creep in on us. He said that if we had been living responsibly day after day, the apartment wouldn't have been in such a mess in the first place. Anyone could have called at any time and dropped by, and we could have had a pretty clean place, but we weren't in the habit of living that way. We had other priorities, and so we were very lazy about the responsibility of keeping up the place where we live.

I really learned from this. I guess I had to hear right from God that it was irresponsible and dangerous to let sloth start to creep into our lives in any way because ultimately it will get into our prayer life. There is a carelessness that can come that we have to be on guard against at all times. Mediocrity will start to creep in very quickly to the point that we don't care. Since we are too busy to pray, we are not being energized so fatigue and weariness will come. We don't have energy because we don't have that Uncreated Energy within us; we're not using the power and energy of the Holy Spirit. There's no joy. We're not striving for perfection. We are lukewarm, and out of this can come compromise, which is very, very dangerous. Jesus had some very serious words about those who are lukewarm. "I know your deeds; I know you are neither cold nor hot. How I wish you were one or the other - hot or cold! But because you are lukewarm, neither hot nor cold, I will spew you out of my mouth!" (Rv 3:15-16)

At a deeper level, sloth will lead us to discouragement, moodiness, and to lows that we can't pull out of after awhile. Discouragement is one of the main weapons of Satan. He loves to use this weapon because He knows it will draw us further and further away from the One who can give us encouragement, affirmation, and hope. This is because our love relationship with God is being undermined. Sloth is very harmful, and ultimately it will paralyze us. Sloth has so many manifestations in our lives that we're not even aware of them. This hiddenness and deception are two of the reasons why it is so deadly.

Sloth leads to depression and an oppressive sorrow because we begin to live our life without God. There's a loss of meaning in life, which leads to spiritual blindness and weakens our will because we're not making choices that require effort. Everything about the spiritual life takes effort; it doesn't come naturally. It's not natural to be a Christian, and it's definitely not natural to be a saint.

Part of the personality of this sin is that it never finishes anything. It never finishes projects. It gets bored and tires very easily. It loses interest easily because it's not motivated. We're not focused on God when this sin gets a hold of us. One interesting thing about sloth is that we can grow up with it and not even realize it. It's like air pollution. It just starts coming into our city more and more and more, and we just live with it. We can start living with sloth almost like it's a friend. Sloth is so deceptive. In our culture today we have microwaves, we don't have to go out and milk the cows, and we don't have to scrub the floors on our hands and knees. We have all these modern conveniences, yet we have less time than ever before. Something is out of order, and it's given tremendous room for sloth to come into our lives.

Again, sloth is deadly because it's deceptive as it manifests itself in busyness, particularly in busyness about good things. One way we can spot it is not so much through all the wonderful things we're doing or even through what we think are necessary things in our everyday lives but through our answers to the following questions: What is happening in my spiritual life? What is happening in my relationship with the Lord? Is spiritual laziness getting in? Am I skipping my prayer time? Am I cutting it short? Or am I just daydreaming or reading it away? We need to check ourselves closely. What is happening primarily with the relationship between God and myself? These questions will help us to spot sloth.

Sloth is a destroyer of love, and when it starts to undermine our relationship with God, it is going to affect our relationship with others as well. Sloth will discourage because sloth is prayerlessness. We're not being energized by love; we're not connecting with God, and so our focus will change to negativity and fault-finding. Have you ever had a wonderful idea and had someone say, "It's not going to work." Sloth discourages others from even trying. We become a pessimist because it's the shortcut. We can sit on the sidelines and say, "Well, I told you it wasn't going to work. Why did you go to all that trouble?" Sloth can lead us into being judgmental. It can bring anger and discontent.

In other words, we can simply stop caring, and it can come about in subtle ways. I remember having a change of superiors in the cloister. I thought the new superior was very nice, but there was one quality about her that I'd never seen in anyone before. She was indifferent. She never got upset; she never got angry; she never would look people in the eye. Maybe she thought it was a virtue to be indifferent or to be that detached. She never had anything to say. She could just walk by as though you weren't standing there. Have you ever had that happen? You're just not present to that other person. I remember saying to the Lord, "I'd rather have her angry with me or even hate me. At least she'd know I'm here." This kind of indifference makes us stop caring. There's nothing quite like it.

Sloth will convince us to settle for a mere avoidance of sin instead of making positive steps to uproot the sin. It can convince us that, "Well, I'm not doing anything to really upset the apple cart. I'm not doing anything to truly offend God." But on the other hand, what am I doing to promote the relationship, to help it grow, and to be more available?

How does sloth show up in myself? Does it show up under the guise of busyness or as something good? We are all busy people, and we're all doing good things, but are we doing the best things? Have we chosen the better portion? Is there a balance here? Does sloth show up in my own life through boredom? Have I stopped listening to homilies? Am I easily distracted? Am I giving my best effort to my work or am I doing slipshod work? Am I too fond of rest? This is not a rest that we need because we're tired. There is an attitude, a spirit of laziness, that can be within us. Is our attitude, "Let somebody else do it"? Has my love grown very lukewarm? Do I have a careless attitude about certain things? Am I procrastinating?

Tardiness can be a manifestation of sloth. I'm not talking about the exceptions but about being late consistently. When I was in college, one of my friends was always late, and my mother said, "Whatever time you are planning on going out, know that they will pick you up thirty minutes later. That's their pattern." That gave me a great deal of peace. It didn't excuse my friends for being late, but it changed the way I could handle it and keep my peace. Tardiness is an offshoot of this sin of sloth because we really don't care enough to show up on time.

My brother has many beautiful virtues, and he is always on time. One time I asked him about that. "You're always on time. How did you get this habit? What motivates you?" He said, "The love and respect for the people I'm going to be with. I owe it to them." He felt it showed disrespect not to be on time. His answer has stuck with me tremendously. Tardiness starts with a lack of charity, as does each of the sins.

Another way we can spot this sin, at least in the beginning, is if we seek excuses to get out of work assignments or studying. Am I a person who doesn't finish the projects I start? Do I have a tendency to leave things unfinished? It might be writing a poem. It might be reading a book. It might be some project around the house or at work. Do I tire of things easily? Do I seek excuses to get out of things?

One of the reasons sloth is so prevalent today is that we are living in a culture of death as Pope John Paul II has said. Sloth is prevalent in a society that lacks passion for truth. If we don't have a passion for truth, we're going to look for things that will make us happy. St. Augustine said, "He who has God has everything, and he who has everything but God has nothing."

In My Spiritual Life

When we get spiritually lazy, all kinds of other sins are going to come in—all the other six to be exact! St. Thomas Aquinas and St. Gregory felt that sloth was the root of many other sins. When we start to shun the spiritual things and anything to do with God and begin to experience them as distasteful, then we will be much more open to the things of the flesh and the world. Then we can get into other sins. In other words, if we're not finding any spiritual pleasure in prayer or in the things of God, we're going to seek those pleasures somewhere else. Many people seek those pleasures in busyness and doing things *for* God, not leaving any time to be *with* God anymore.

119

So this sin of spiritual sloth is very dangerous. It will lead to repugnance, almost disgust, of spiritual things and the work of sanctification in our own souls because it takes too much effort and brings demands that we just don't want to look at. The idea of entering the narrow gate is very saddening and repugnant. We don't want to work at sanctity, or becoming a saint, or becoming a kind, loving, generous, patient person. Sloth keeps us from seeking and achieving perfection. We're not really very interested.

One time I was struggling with sloth and had not been in prayer much. My spiritual director was a very holy man and caught it right away. He told me, "This is not the saintly way to act. You should act this way if you want to become a saint." Right away I picked up on that word saint, and I remember saying, "Saint? Who cares about being a saint?" I was so involved in whatever the problem was to even care about being a saint. This is what sloth does to us. It takes us away from God's perfect will for us, which is for us to become a saint. If we stop praying with intensity and stop making the connection with God, then our love of God's will for us will start to grow lukewarm within us, and we won't be concerned about sanctity anymore. We will become more concerned about what is happening in our little life than with what God wants to do in our lives. Our own personal sins will take us down so that we won't be able to be used in the powerful burden-bearing ministry that God is calling us to as prayer warriors.

Spiritual sloth will tempt us to omit our spiritual duties. For example, the Examination of Conscience can become annoying, and so we start to skip it and our sins are no longer accounted for to God. Going to Reconciliation gets less frequent, and if we do go, we stay on the surface with the same old things. There's a tendency for slothfulness in our journaling because journaling can be a labor for some. It's a discipline. It's not something we do naturally.

Maybe we won't totally stop our praying, but we will give into the temptation to shorten our prayer by five, ten, or fifteen minutes. This is a real temptation when spiritual sloth enters into our lives this way because in the spiritual life there are times of dryness. There are the desert times. There are times of tremendous aridity. Teresa of Avila experienced fifteen to twenty years of tremendous aridity. Often she would shake her hourglass, trying to make her prayer time go by faster. But she didn't walk away. She remained faithful. She persevered. She didn't get into spiritual sloth. When that breakthrough came, she became one of the greatest mystics that the Church has ever seen. We might not have an hourglass to shake, but we have watches, and we can fidget. We know all sorts of ways to help the time to go faster, such as reading or daydreaming away our prayer time.

Sloth will show up in our attitude while we are praying. For example, are we praying as a matter of routine because we have to? What's our motive? Do we pray in a lazy posture that's conducive to slipping off to sleep? St. Ignatius says to pray in the posture that is best for us. Kneeling might be best for someone, while it could be very uncomfortable and a terrible distraction for another person. If we find that we pray in a lazy posture and wake up an hour later, we need to make a change. If we find ourselves praying halfheartedly, hurrying to get through our prayers to get them over with, or making resolutions that we never keep, sloth is working within.

Sometimes when we're going through the purification times, boredom can set in. We have to be careful that we don't give in to sloth and stop persevering in prayer because the tendency is to want to run. We have very sophisticated ways of running. For myself, I used to talk on the telephone all the time; I had to call someone. Then the Lord showed me, "You are running. That's not the priority here. That's not the one thing necessary." We have all sort of other things to do.

When spiritual sloth creeps into our lives, it will destroy our love for God. It will rob us, first of all, of our hunger and thirst for God. The Rosary can get boring. Prayer can get boring. We may think, "Oh, I've read that Scripture so many times. I don't get anything out of it. I've read this book. I've heard this saint being quoted. It's boring. Why should I spend time in front of the Blessed Sacrament anymore? He never says anything to me. It's boring." These can all be temptations to spiritual sloth, and it will destroy our love and our love relationship with the Lord. Spiritual sloth can bring about depression because we're not receiving life or peace; we're not being touched by God. It saddens the soul very deeply and heaviness comes. Everything is difficult.

Sloth will encourage us to seek spiritual gratification, which is usually seeking our own will and even trying to convince God that our way is best. If God doesn't do things our way then we say,

"Well, it's just not God's will." See how sloth can cover up truth? It can conceal. We can so easily say, "Well, I don't think God really wanted that," but deep down, we know we didn't get close enough to Him to even find out what He did want because sloth is keeping us apart. There seems to be a great deal of pleasure in doing our own thing, while doing God's will takes too much energy. I know people who prefer not to go into prayer because they're afraid they might find out what God says, and it would take effort to do it. It's like the concept that ignorance is bliss, but really it isn't.

There are some people with the gift of Knowledge and awareness of God's will for them, who follow God's will but complain about how hard it is. They are like little children who have to follow their parents, complaining loudly and dragging their feet all the time. They may complain that this is not their preference, and so they don't have any joy. This is one way that sloth will manifest itself. They follow God's will only because they know that this is what He wants, and so they "have to do it." They are going to do it solely out of obedience, but they are not going to like it. So there isn't any joy, and it doesn't get them anywhere.

It's not that He has stopped loving us, but we are no longer connecting or receiving from Him. "I'm just too busy, Lord. I'm too busy serving You right now." We can get too busy in our families, also. Parents particularly have to be very careful as they can get so busy running the household and taking the children back and forth to activities that the beautiful, intimate time with each other gets lessened and lessened, and there can develop into problems in their marriage.

John of the Cross tells us that sloth will show up in our spiritual life according to where we are on the spiritual journey. Beginners usually come into the spiritual life with a lot of consolations. This is how God baits us, and when God starts to shift and takes us deeper and strips away all the excess that we bring in, we can get very slothful because we don't like that. All of a sudden, prayer is distasteful. It's boring. We're not receiving those warm fuzzies, and the tendency is to give up and walk away, particularly in beginners, because beginners only want to continue what makes them feel good. We may have heard people say, "Well, I don't go to Mass anymore. I don't really get anything out of it." That's a beginner: "If there's nothing in it for me, then I'm not going to do it." We have to be careful of sloth in our prayer because if we're going to grow in maturity, then we have to grow beyond this desire for the easy way.

John of the Cross said that as God leads souls through the dark night (which purifies them for true agape love) and they get closer to the Cross, this is where most people turn around and walk away. They don't have that maturity, they don't have that energy, and they don't have that love connection with God. He said they don't want to go through the thicket where the thorns and suffering are in order to come into deeper union. Sloth becomes very deadly in the spiritual life because it will try to prevent us from union with Jesus Christ Crucified, which is the most important union for all of us because all power and wisdom comes from the Cross. This is where sin is totally put to death.

It will seem costly to do God's will until we begin to fall more and more in love with Him. Then we will strive to become more like Jesus and do only and always what pleases the Father, which will bring us tremendous joy. When Jesus hung on the Cross, He wasn't in any ministry like He had ever been in before, but the energy and the discipline to stay there and surrender to God's will was a tremendous labor. We need to ask ourselves if this is manifested in our prayer lives.

The sin of sloth is probably the most common and deadliest sin in the Church today. It is so effective and deceptive. It keeps us busy, busy, busy about many things but lazy about our spiritual life, lazy about our relationship with God, lazy about the one thing that is necessary. We are so busy doing good things that we are too busy to pray, too busy to have our priorities straight, and too busy to seek first the Kingdom of God. We are too tired to pray, and we think, "God will understand because I'm busy doing good things for Him."

Spiritual Warfare

One of the deadliest things about sloth is that it can cause delay. It can delay God's timing. It can delay God's plan for us, and it can hinder others, including ourselves, from going forward. We can be blocks to others as we are not encouraging or cheering them on. The Lord let me understand in prayer a long time ago that this delay is definitely of the enemy. But sloth is of the

123

enemy. It's one of the dragon's heads. One time the Lord showed me that Satan knows he cannot stop this call that God had brought me out of the convent for, but one of his tactics will be to delay it. Delay, delay, delay. So have you ever tried to get somewhere or do something and you're just constantly delayed? After four or five times, you finally begin to realize, "I'm running interference here. This is not normal. There is a spirit of sloth here."

Sloth stifles growth, it stifles new ideas, and it can undermine those who want to try new things to improve a family or community. Sloth can be very divisive as it works against unity, and eventually it will draw us away from family members and community. It breeds isolationism, and ultimately it weakens the whole group.

Remedies

Gift of the Holy Spirit: Knowledge

The gift of Knowledge is the main gift of the Holy Spirit to help us combat this sin of sloth. Knowledge is a gift that God gave us to know what He knows. It is a gift to have the mind of Jesus. St. Paul said, "Do not conform yourselves to this age but be transformed by the renewal of your mind so that you may judge what is God's will, what is good, pleasing, and perfect" (Rom 12:2). Unless we have this gift of Knowledge, we will not have the full discernment of what God's perfect will is. We want to know His perfect will, not His permissive will. Many people live out of what God's permits because they don't ask Him what is His perfect will. The gift of Knowledge lets us know His perfect will so that we can move in that gift and come into deep union.

This great gift of Knowledge will help us see beyond the moment, so we can see that our busyness and indifference are jeopardizing our relationship with God. It will help us see where apathy is setting in and destroying our relationship with God. It will show us that we are not being fed or nurtured; we're not learning or communicating with God.

Knowledge is pure gift. It comes out of our intuition. It's a holy knowledge of things that God has created and of what God wants, and knowledge will give us a power and an energy to do His will. Theologians call Knowledge "the science of the saints" as the saints had this gift operating within them tremendously. The saints weren't afraid of that labor of love, they weren't afraid of the cost, and they worked at it. They had knowledge of God's will and knowledge of the truth, and they had a passion for it. Intercessors need this gift of Knowledge to learn God's way and His plan that puts us on that holy path to perfection. Some of the saints say that the gift of Knowledge is almost like a second conversion.

The gift of Knowledge is a tremendous gift of power because it lets us know what God knows. Knowledge in itself is power. Satan knows that, and he wants us to remain ignorant of what God knows. The sin of sloth can keep us ignorant; it can keep us away from God and His knowledge which will give us power over the enemy. Prayer warriors need to know what God wants us to know.

Solomon said, "Vanity of vanities. All things are vanity" (Eccl 1:2). This is the gift of Knowledge working. St. Paul understood it so well when he said, "I have come to rate all as loss in the light of the surpassing knowledge of my Lord, Jesus Christ" (Phil 3:8). St. Francis of Assisi also had this gift of Knowledge operating to a very high degree. He obviously had God's love of creation; everything that God created spoke to him of God. The saints tell us that with this gift of Knowledge the whole world become a cathedral. We can see God's handiwork in all things. We begin to fall more and more in love with God and everything He has made. This will direct us to a very deep level of detachment where we become very attached to God. Knowledge will give us the courage and energy to always want to do all things to please and thank and praise God.

One time the Lord taught me about detachment. He gave me an image of Himself and myself walking together, hand in hand. I had a few other attachments in my free hand. So I was walking hand and hand with God, but still hanging onto some other things, and He said, "Let go." I said, "Let go?" He said, "Better yet, just take hold of My other hand." He's a master psychologist, isn't He? Try that some time! Holding God with both hands swings our bodies around face to face, with Him. We're focused on Him. We're right on track! He really wants us to be fully focused on Him. As sin diminishes in our lives, the turning gets easier as we turn more and more to face Him right away.

Knowledge gives us the prayer power that we need so much. "Never cease praying" (1Thes 5:17). Nothing could come against sloth any better than to pray without ceasing. "At every opportunity pray in the Spirit" (Eph 6:18-19). "Whoever hold out to the end will escape death" (Mt 10:22). "By patient endurance, you will save your lives" (Lk 21:19). So we can't give up. We can't give up.

In the earlier days when this call was starting to come together, there were so many ups and downs. The enemy was constantly doing everything he could to stop it. We still hadn't moved out to our center yet. People were kind of coming and going, and it was hard to gather a community together because we didn't have a place to put them. So they'd be here for awhile, and then they were gone. After awhile I was getting discouraged. I was starting to think, "Oh Lord, how long? How long am I going to be out here by myself? How long am I going to take this buffeting constantly by the enemy? How long am I going to be without the community that I need so desperately? How long, O Lord?" My thoughts even went a little bit further—"I wonder if I should go back to the cloister." That's exactly where the enemy wanted me to go.

I remember when I first wondered if I should go back to the cloister. It came on a Sunday morning. I lived right on the church grounds in a hermitage. It was Father's Day, and the church was packed. The priest started a beautiful homily about the Heavenly Father, and all of a sudden, he stopped and changed the course of his homily. He totally changed the subject, and said, "Don't give up. Do you hear me? Someone out there is ready to give up. Don't give up!"

Oh my goodness! I heard that. It gave me an adrenaline shot and that energy came back. God's Word came right into my heart, and I was energized. I knew it was the Lord, and I was never tempted to give up again. I always praise and thank God for that priest's obedience to the Spirit. The priest later told me, "I had no idea who I was talking to, but the power of the Spirit was so strong that I forgot my whole homily." So that was a Father's Day that neither one of us will ever forget.

Words from the Cross

We are all called to be victims of God's most merciful love, and so we are driven to the Cross more and more. Our consecration, our commitment to live Jesus and His Cross, will truly strengthen us from the attack of sloth. With Jesus' sixth word, "It is finished" (Jn 19:30), He is cutting right through sloth. He persevered. He stayed with it. This is intercession at its best. "I have given You glory on earth by finishing the work that You gave Me to do" (Jn 17:4). This labor of love should be very familiar to intercessors.

There are wonderful fruits that come forth after the struggle with sloth. Joy is restored. There's no joy like it because we're free. There's a tremendous faith in us that we can do it. We can be faithful because God can give us the grace. We can do it everyday.

Jesus finished the work the Father had given Him to do. He persevered in it through thick or thin. We can take one day at a time and persevere in our work. Sometimes that's the only grace that we seem to have - to persevere. Can we persevere in our intercession, particularly when we don't see anything happening? Can we persevere when the Cross is heavy, and we want to walk away, pack our bags, and run? We may do that many times mentally, but there is a fidelity that comes against sloth. We can choose to be faithful and persevere in our tasks. If we want to be busy about something, we can be busy about the work that the Father has given us to do—our sanctification.

Sloth is one of the more hidden sins. It is tremendously deceptive and concealed. We need to look at it to see where it is prevalent in our lives so we can come against it. Along with Jesus, we want to be able to say, "Father, I have finished the work that You gave me to do." Not the work that I am choosing to do. Not all the things that I want to be running around about, but the work that You have given me to do. Jesus' main work was redemptive. It was intercession, connecting souls to the Father. So we have been called to a glorious, holy work. Sloth is going to try to undermine it, to stop it, or at least to delay it. "All things work together for good of those who have been called according to His decree" (Rom 8:28).

Virtues:
Love, Obedience

There are always more than one virtue that will help us counteract these Capital Sins. The dominant virtue here will be love manifested through the sacrifice of obedience. Prompt obedience to God is very helpful in fighting sloth. As soon as we understand what He is saying, then we should immediately do it. If we put off obeying, we are procrastinating and giving in to this sin. Procrastination is dominant in our society. We can do everything in love.

Perseverance can overcome tepidity. This is very important for intercessors and prayer warriors because we are in a ministry that when we pray for others we are taking on sin. Once we can get rid of our own personal sins, then we will be better able to take on sin with Jesus for others and become victim lambs. St. Paul said "In my own flesh I make up for what is lacking in the sufferings of Christ for the sake of His Body, the Church" (Col 1:24). We can stand in the gap and know the power of interceding and connecting God and man again.

Additional Helps

We can exercise our will, resist sloth, and choose to be on a heaven-bound path. We can get on the right path and choose it. It's like whenever we take a trip. We get out the map and look at the options. There are different ways of getting from one place to another. In other words, we need to make the firm resolution to choose to be a pilgrim to the Holy Land.

St. Thomas said that the more we think about spiritual goods, the more pleasing they will become to us and sloth will die away because we've changed our focus towards God. We can conquer spiritual sloth by a real love of God and making choices that please God. Jesus said, "I have come to ignite a fire on the earth. How I wish that blaze were ignited!" (Lk 12:49) We can make a choice not to accept mediocrity in our spiritual life or be lulled into complacency. We can make choices to be true and faithful to our daily prayer and to persevere in developing a relationship with God. Perseverance is key in fighting this particular sin.

The spiritual writers tell us that daily sacrifices of some sort will restore vigor to our spiritual lives. The Little Flower learned this very beautifully. When her zeal, that fire, would start to go out, she would offer sacrifices. She referred to her little sacrifices throughout the day as straws. She said each little sacrifice was like a little straw that she would feed into the flame of God within her, and it would fan the flame. One little straw, then another little straw, and another until her zeal and fire for God and His people would come back. Feeding our spiritual lives with little spiritual sacrifices all day long, knowingly and willingly, is a great practice to come against sloth.

We have learned to take our distractions to the Lord. We don't struggle with distractions or try to get them out of our mind. That takes a lot of energy and time away from our prayer time, so we simply turn the distraction into a prayer. If we're distracted about something, we take it to the Lord and talk to Him about it. Somehow He will show us something in the distraction that He wants us to know or pray about. The main thing is that we're connecting with God.

One wonderful experience in prayer that began with a distraction happened when I was making a retreat. The retreat master's name was Father David, and his name was anointed for me. In prayer time, Father David came to my mind, and instead of treating it as a distraction, which I really felt it was, I asked the Lord, "Why am I all of a sudden thinking of Father David? Do I know anyone named David?" The Lord didn't bring anything to my mind, so I asked, "Lord, do You know anyone named David?" because the distraction was still there. He said yes and brought David the shepherd boy to mind. He started showing me David playing his harp and writing those beautiful psalms. The Lord said, "I would like you to be my harp so that I can play and sing any song upon your heart that I choose." It became a beautiful prayer period. So don't struggle with distractions. The enemy loves that. We can always ask God to remove the distractions, but if it doesn't go, then take it to the Lord, dialogue with Him about it, and let that become the beginning of your prayer. It can be a beautiful springboard in our prayer.

We can make a conscious effort to get rid of our faults. There is a purification process, a laboring, that takes place as we try to get away from sloth. It takes effort, and it can be costly to really be free of venial sins and all the little imperfections. We want to be totally with God. So we need to make resolutions or plans on how we are going to combat this sinful area within us. Our resolutions should be concrete; we don't want to be vague. One of the enemy's strategies is for us to generalize and to do it tomorrow—mañana. So act promptly.

We need to keep a schedule (not a very detailed schedule, but something that is reasonable for our lifestyle and obligations), and then immediately do what we tend to put off. We need to walk right into those things that we have a tendency to procrastinate about. Our choices are so important. We don't want to be fooled into complacency. We can choose to exert our will and not take the easy way out.

St. Paul knew this very well. He said, "You are my children, and you put me back into labor pains until Christ is formed in you" (Gal 4:19). He was taking on sin; he was going through the birthing process. Paul wasn't dealing with just his own sins, but he was dealing also with the sins of those he was trying to shepherd so that they could come forth reborn in Jesus.

Our commitment to daily prayer can be sacrificial. If so, we can begin with short periods and as we get more energy, we will find more ways and time slots when we can pray. The enemy would like us to begin with big time frames for prayer. He likes exaggeration. We have a tendency to be overly generous each year at Lent: "I'm going to pray an hour. I'm going to make a holy hour every day." That's nice, but did God really ask this of us? Did He really want it? Because if He didn't, if we're being inspired by the enemy, then two or three days into Lent, something may come up, and we can't keep our holy hour. Then we begin to feel guilty and beat ourselves to death because we feel we have let God down, but He never asked for this in the first place. The enemy did. This happens quite often as people begin to pray, so we have to be careful. We need to discern what God is asking of us. Does He want fifteen minutes of prayer each day, every day? He'd rather have that than nothing.

As you begin this examination of conscience,
become aware of God's deep love for you.
Ask for God's light to surround you
so that you may see your soul as God sees it.
Pray for the willingness and the grace
to desire to become more like Jesus.

EXAMINATION OF CONSCIENCE—SLOTH

In general
Do I have an inordinate love of rest and inactivity?
   Do I omit or neglect any physical or spiritual duties?
   Do I feel sluggishness of mind that prevents me from
      beginning tasks that I need to do?
   Do I feel a repugnance in having to work or put forth any
      effort?
   Do I have a tendency towards idleness?
Do I feel an oppressive sorrow that weighs me down so that I
want to do nothing?
   Am I moody, discouraged, gloomy, or depressed?
   Do I have a distaste for life in general?
Do I feel a voluntary disgust for spiritual things and the work of
sanctification because of all the effort and self-discipline they
demand?
Does my sin of sloth manifest itself in busyness, as I attempt to
hide and to fill the place that only God can fill with anything
else but Him?

How am I glorifying God in my work?
Do I fulfill my duties promptly, carefully, and to the best of my
ability?
   Do I avoid duties that are my job but are tasks that I don't like?
   Do I find myself doing other things so that I don't have time to
      perform an unpleasant job?
   Do I procrastinate in fulfilling tasks that I know are my
      responsibility?
Do I have a tendency towards sloth?
   Can I recognize any beginnings of sloth manifested in
      unconcern, carelessness, and negligence?
   Is sloth hidden in my life? Have I become accustomed to it?
   Do I refuse to put all my effort into what I am doing?

Has my sloth progressed to a dislike for any serious physical and mental labor?

Do I work at times when I should be praying? Do I pray when I should be working?

How can I better glorify God in my work?

How am I glorifying God in my prayer and spiritual duties?

Where is sloth most prevalent in my spiritual journey?

Am I faithful to my daily prayer, listening to the Lord, and journaling?

Do I truly hunger and thirst to hear from the Lord each day?

Do I treasure each word from the Lord and reflect upon them in my heart?

Do I pay close attention to how the Lord is directing me in my prayer and journaling?

Do I become weary and flee from prayer when it seems empty, dry, and mundane?

Do I fill all my prayer time with rote prayers because listening to what the Lord has to say and journaling seem like too much work?

Do I allow the silence within me to be cluttered with busyness, stray thoughts, etc.?

Am I slipping into complacency regarding my sins, skipping my examination of conscience and avoiding the Sacrament of Reconciliation?

Do I avoid searching for meaning in my life, leading me to fear and avoid God's love?

Do I find myself doing things so that I don't have time to pray?

Do I hurry through my prayer time in order to get it over with?

Do I become easily distracted in prayer?

What steps have I taken to ensure that I stay attentive to the Lord?

Am I wearied and disgusted by all the work and effort the spiritual journey takes?

Does this cause me to omit my spiritual duties or to perform them negligently?

Do I resent the time that my prayer and spiritual duties take up?

Am I mediocre and lazy in my prayer and spiritual study habits, doing just enough to get by?

How am I glorifying God through my participation in Community and Family Life?

How does my weakness in this area of sloth affect my family and community?

  Does my slothful and careless attitude hinder and hold others back on their journey?

  Where does my community or family need me to put forth more effort and zeal?

Do I live at the expense of others?

  Do I grumble or complain when things are not comfortable for me?

How am I responsible for unity in my community and family?

  Do I participate fully in communal or family prayer? Am I giving it my all?

  What is my attitude regarding communal and family prayer?

  Do I obey promptly, cheerfully, and with my whole heart, mind, and soul?

How does my recreation glorify the Lord?

The Call to Perfection

Am I actively seeking perfection? If so, how?

  Am I half-hearted and tepid in my love and service of God?

  Am I comfortable being average with no real desire to improve or correct my faults?

  How does sloth cause me to not welcome or cooperate with purification in my life?

  How do I resist correcting my faults?

  How am I actively working to raise my standards to become more like Jesus?

  What is robbing me of my appetite and interest in God?

Is there a sin area in my life that I am not ready to give up yet?

Does my sin of sloth cause me so much sorrow that I turn to worldly goods and pleasures of the body (lust) to provide gratification rather than turning to God alone?

How do I resist the temptation to sloth in my spiritual journey?

  What acts of mortification do I practice in my life, and what is my attitude about them?

How has my intimacy with the Lord grown over the past 6 months?

How often throughout the day do I turn my heart towards the Lord?

The ministry of intercession

Does this ministry of intercession and carrying the Cross seem like too much of a bother?

Do I complain when I don't feel pleasure and gratification or when I don't receive thanks?

Do I actively study to learn more about this charism?

Do I respond to this call to be an intercessor half-heartedly?

Where am I growing lax, lukewarm, and losing my enthusiasm and zeal in living this lifestyle of intercession?

Choose two or three items from above where strengthening is needed the most. Take the time to journal them with the Lord. Then make a resolution on how you are going to cooperate with the Lord to combat this sin area in your life. Review this resolution plan daily.

Chapter 7

Avarice

Avarice (also known as covetousness or greed) is an inordinate love of and desire for worldly goods, which includes the desire and love for riches, possessions, money, knowledge, and an inordinate love of possessing. It goes against our reason. It's immoderate.

St. Paul tells us that the love of money is the root of all evil (1Tm 6:10). That's a pretty powerful statement that he's making because we know pride itself is the root of all the evils, and he is saying the love of money is the root of all evil. So when we pray about it, somehow the love of money is tied into pride as well. St. Thomas Aquinas said, "Covetousness is the root of all actual sins" (*A Tour of the Summa*, 84-1). So theologians are placing a great deal of emphasis on the deadliness of this sin and the root of it. Christian tradition ranks the capital sin of avarice second only to pride.

Avarice comes against two of the commandments. The First Commandment says "I am the Lord your God; you shall not have strange gods before me." We are not to have any idols. We are not to have anything before God, including ourselves. This sin sets oneself up before God because it doesn't make God its treasure. It serves itself. It in itself becomes a treasure. Theologians tell us that a person indulging in avarice makes his or her hidden treasure a god and will sacrifice everything for it: their time, strength, and sometimes even their family. Avarice can even go so far as to encourage a person to sacrifice their eternity. This is frightening, isn't it? We can't serve God and money. Sin always comes down to our choice.

The Tenth Commandment says, "You shall not covet your neighbors' goods." This commandment forbids greed, passion for riches, and the desire to hoard up all these earthly goods (particularly for oneself) without any kind of limit. Maybe we don't have something, but we want it, and this is where our focus is. This desire will motivate us tremendously. It will take us in one direction or the other. A desire for riches and the things of this world will lead us right into Satan's camp. St. Thomas Aquinas tells us that avarice becomes a mortal sin when we will do anything necessary to possess riches. We live in a culture that is filled with avarice. Several years ago I asked my sister-in-law what she thought was the number one problem in the world. I was amazed at her answer. Without batting an eyelash she said, "Selfishness." There's a lot of wisdom in her statement.

Avarice is very possessive. It's a perversion of our need for security and our basic right to possess. If we are insecure and fearful, we can get the octopus mentality. We think we need to provide for ourselves, so we reach out and grab this and grab that in many areas. We may let go of one thing but we grasp onto something else. God often shows us one area and tells us, "Let it go. You're hanging on to this; you're clinging." It's very difficult to let go of everything. It takes the love power of the Cross to do that. Avarice clings to things because it's very selfish. Avarice comes out of not having a good, solid relationship with the Father, who is *the* Provider.

When I came home from the cloister, I lived in a little apartment for some time. I knew that down the line eventually there would be a place where He would provide for community because God had been showing me. We would need to have things to fill a house wherever that was going to be. People started giving us different things, so we were storing these things in peoples' attics. Anyone who would loan us an attic, we would store things there.

One day I heard about some people who were moving to California and were putting everything in their house up for auction. Boy, my antennae went up on that! I thought, "This is great. It would be wonderful to have a washer and a dryer, Lord." That's something that I could never afford and no one had ever given us a washer and dryer. We've been given a couch or a chair here and there, but no one had ever given us a washer and a dryer.

So my friend and I went to this auction. I had never been to an auction before. We were waiting for the bigger stuff, the washer and dryer, so we had to stay there all morning while they auctioned off all this little stuff first. Finally around one o'clock they were going to get to the bigger things in the house, and the first thing was the washer and the dryer. I thought, "Oh, this is wonderful!" I had been praying, "Be sure to let me know, Lord, what kind of a bid I should make." The minute the auctioneer announced it was going to be the washer and the dryer, the Lord spoke to me. I'll never forget it as long as I live. I was so shocked. He said very lovingly, kindly, gently, but firmly and clearly, "Nadine, don't be a squirrel." I thought, "Pardon me?" And again, very gently, "Don't be a squirrel." I said, "What do you mean?" He said, "You don't need that right now. Squirrels hoard things up that they don't need. They store. Don't be a squirrel." I said, "In other words, You're saying now (four hours later—I didn't say that to Him, but I thought it) we can't get the washer and dryer." He said, "That's right. You don't need it now." So I told my friend, "We have to go." She said, "Oh, no. They're going to auction them off right now." He had already started asking for the bids. I said, "No, we have to go." We left. When we got out the door I told her what the Lord had said. I think He was trying to talk to me about this sin of avarice that I was ready to fall into in a big way. So don't be a squirrel. Don't think that we always need to provide for ourselves.

So we are talking about attachment. When we refer to money and possessions, it can include other things like the positions we hold, always wanting to climb the ladder of success. We live in a culture that's filled with greed, possessing, and concern for reputation. We can be greedy about knowledge. We can read book after book after book because we want to be the first one to know something. This feeds into pride. So avarice has many other aspects other than just money.

Avarice can bring about false attachments to one's home, to what one does for entertainment, to books, to furniture, and to anything that's precious. We're not saying not to be attached or not to take care of the things that God has given to us, but there can be a false attachment where we're clinging to them. We're possessive and God help anybody if they try to take it or remove it or even need it or use it. Sometimes we think we're not attached at all and think we're quite free when really we're not.

There was a sister in a cloister who had little straight pins. We carried little pincushions on us for pinning, and she always wanted the straight pins that had the little pink colored heads on top. That got to be quite an attachment for her, which she didn't even realize until they were missing one day. We can get attached to a certain place where we're going sit every Sunday in church. It can show up in everything. It's everywhere. The

Holy Spirit is trying to make us aware that these are all things that are not of God. These are not things we would find in the life of Jesus or Mary.

Why is avarice harmful? Money in itself is not evil, but *the love* of money is the root of all evil. God has said, "You shall have no other gods before me," and money and possessions have very much become gods, particularly in our nation. Avarice shows up in crime. It shows up in how we use our credit cards. If we don't have the money, we just have to use that little piece of plastic. It has shown up in the big corporations, and it shows up in the tremendous discrepancy between the rich and the poor. Money and possessions have become an idol because when we are dependent upon money and things, it becomes very harmful. We leave that spiritual childhood behind, and we're not dependent upon God, especially as Father, to provide. When the Father spoke to me as I was being called out of the cloister, He said He would provide everything I needed but not everything I desired. Now I see that He was talking about this sin. And He does provide everything we need.

Avarice will almost end up possessing us if we start to make money or possessions our god because then we think we need to have more and more. It's in a terrible no-win situation, isn't it? God created all things to be good, but we have taken so much of what He has created to be good and started to worship it as our god. God gave me a tremendous Scripture years ago as a new convert, and it just burned into my soul. "What profit would a man show if he were to gain the whole world and destroy himself in the process?" (Mt 16:26; Mk 8:36; Lk 9:25) I remember the first time I ever heard that as a Catholic it just pierced my heart. I thought, "Oh my God, don't ever let me get to where I have to possess, possess, and suffer the loss of my own soul." What would it profit a man?

Avarice leads to many other sins, as do all the other Capital Sins. They lead right back into the other sins and interconnect. Avarice is a sinfulness that lies in going too far to acquire and keep possessions. It's out of balance. It spawns a host of other sins like cheating, lying, perjury, and violence. It leads to betrayal of friends, which was the sin of Judas. It blinds us especially to the reality of heaven. We can become restless and very dissatisfied because we always want to push on to some place where we're not. Our hearts can get very hardened. So we have to be able to spot avarice because if we are not aware, we can follow the spirit of the world without even knowing it.

What Avarice Looks Like in Me

Now we'll try to get a little more personal. How does this apply to my life? How does it show up in myself? One way could be through materialism, the tendency to have to acquire earthly goods. Materialism is everywhere. When we speak of the spirit of the world, which is in the power of Satan, we are speaking of materialism and money, which are false gods. We have become so accustomed to a way of life. We live in the world, but the challenge is to be in the world but not of it. Avarice might show up in my desire to have something that I don't have. Just the desiring something can start to lead me away from God. It is not going to sever me from God, but it clouds the relationship and draws me away from giving my whole self to the Lord.

We had a beautiful older sister in the cloister. We were talking about what we had left behind when we entered the cloister. Most of us were talking about it with great joy because we had received so much more. This sister had a sadness to her about what she had left behind. Actually it wasn't about something she had but something she had always desired. All her life and all her convent life she had always wanted a fur coat. I thought, "Oh my, Lord, it's a shame she didn't go out and get an extra job and buy the fur coat so she could have walked away from it." Yet she clung to this desire all these years. She probably wouldn't have liked it anyway and would have been very happy to give it to the Lord, but the fact that she couldn't walk away from that desire clouded her relationship with the Lord. The desire to have something that she couldn't have possessed her. So we have to watch these desires. They're just as deadly as the actual possessing because even the desires can start to possess us.

Because avarice is a self-centered sin, it robs community and family of resources. In other words, we can get very greedy and not want to share something we've read, something that's happened to us in prayer, or not want to share a particular gift that we have. If even one or two members in a family or a community hold back what God has given to them, they are robbing the rest of

139

the people of what God has given them to share. This is hoarding it, clinging to it, and keeping it just for ourselves—that's avarice.

When this sin is operating within us, there is a tendency to exercise ownership. We can become strongly attached to what we already have, and our attitude about it can get very immature. "Mine. It's mine." This is an attachment. We can be attached to our own opinions. We can be attached to almost anything, can't we? Again, there's that octopus dimension within us that wants to reach out and cling to something. There can be false attachments to our homes and amusements: "I have to see this particular TV program. I need to have this particular book. I need to have this particular kind of furniture." There's nothing wrong in having it, but if our attitude is, "God help anyone if they take it away from me," then we are in danger. If we have a special statue, and it gets broken, we can see how attached we are.

Sometimes we don't know how attached we are to something until someone takes it or we can't find it or someone breaks it. Then we begin to realize, "I am attached to that. I didn't realize it." God wants us to be free, totally free. It isn't that He doesn't want us to have things, but we need to be attached to Him, not things.

We once saw a video about the stages of human development and growth, and I remember that one of the terrible two's favorites words is "mine." People in families, and especially those of us in community who are under vows of poverty, have to be very careful we don't get clingy and possessive of anything. Possessiveness is directly opposed to holding all things in common. Avarice can come in through the tiniest little things. "It's my pen. Where is my pen?" In other words, avarice is not just having to have something, but it's not wanting to share what we do have. It's attachment.

Avarice can show up in our own lives through an over-concern for our economic security. We have to be very careful of that. We need a certain amount of money to live and support those who are in our care, but we have to be careful that we don't get so overly concerned that we are not dependent upon God to provide. Once we lose God's peace and start to worry, we know that we have gotten into some of the tastings of this particular sin.

Avarice can lead us to forgetting about the poor and our obligations to them. We can get so concerned about what we think we need or what we think we don't have that we can forget that we still have to be concerned about others who have less than we do. I've heard missionaries tell stories about the missions they have been in, very poor little islands or countries where there is hardly anything to eat. Yet when they would visit, usually the children would want to share some of their bread with them. Whatever they had, they wanted to share. Isn't that beautiful? They were that free and that childlike to share the little they had.

Avarice can show up in our own personal lives if we have a need within us to be the very first to know something. Have you ever had that tendency? Someone says a little bit of news and you have a twinge inside, "How come I didn't know that first?" We may not want to hear anything secondhand. In avarice there's a need and a drive to possess that little bit of knowledge first.

Avarice can show up when we crave the good opinion of others, the good opinion of community, or the good opinion of those in authority. We can fall into a dishonesty and compromise. We can conceal, cover up, and be hypocritical. We see this a lot in the business world, too. We want the approval of those in authority, and we can do things that are not right in order to get that approval.

In My Spiritual Life

How does avarice show up in my spiritual life? John of the Cross says that it shows up in beginners as being very unhappy because we're not receiving the consolations and spiritual things that we had hoped for. There are usually many consolations in the beginning of our spiritual journey. God knows how to bait and lure us, but as He tries to bring us into a deeper maturity and relationship with the Giver, we get greedy. A childishness starts to come out in us. We may begin to immerse ourselves in spiritual reading rather than striving after mortification, detachment, and the disciplines of the spiritual life. If reading good spiritual books is all we are doing in our spiritual lives, it can be a way of greed for us. It's also a way of running.

We can become very attached to religious practices, devotions, and possessions and not want to share them with anyone. We may be more attached to them than who they represent—the Lord. So there is spiritual avarice here, a spiritual possessiveness, and greed.

141

I had a dear friend who was like a second mother to me before I went into the convent. She was a very beautiful spiritual woman. The first time I went into her home, she took me into her bedroom which was just packed with things. There were statues all over the place and rosaries hanging everywhere. It looked like a church-goods store. I felt smothered. I asked a priest who knew her quite well about it, "What is it? There's something strange. Why does she need all those things for a healthy spiritual life?" He said, "You will often find this in newcomers, beginners in the religious life. They want this, they want that. It's a spiritual immaturity. As she grows more in the Lord and becomes accustomed to His riches, she will start to let these things go. They will start to bother her. Give her about six months and look at her bedroom again." That's exactly what happened. One by one, certain things started to disappear. They were bothering her. She wanted more simplicity. She was getting closer to God now, and her room reflected that. She was getting closer to the Gift Himself, and she could let some of these things go. The special things that really meant something to her stayed, but a lot of this extra stuff started disappearing.

We may have become so attached to religious practices that God may be saying, "I love it when you do that, but not if you're putting it first before listening to Me or doing your other obligations or duties." When I was in the cloister, we were required to say the Rosary. The sisters did pray the Rosary, but when the rule got changed, we had freedom whether or not to say the Rosary. We loved it because now we could pray the Rosary the way the Lord was leading us. It set us free to listen to God. Contemplatives want to listen to God. So we still prayed the Rosary, but we totally reversed it. "Lord, You show us how to pray this Rosary. We want to hear from You now. What are Your intentions? What are Your desires?" It totally reversed the prayer and set us free.

This is what I mean. If things, even good devotions, are starting to possess us, then we need to take that to the Lord and ask Him, "Lord, how do You want me to handle this? This is my favorite novena. This is my favorite devotion. Am I attached to it? Do You want something else instead?" We always have to be ready to move on with the Holy Spirit. He can shift gears. He can lead us this way, and then we might outgrow that because He is leading us in another way. We want to be sure that we are free.

Avarice can manifest itself in our difficulty in depending on God alone. We can have an attachment to our good works. We may think that if we do this and that then we're going to have a wonderful list that God can check off when we go through that gate. "These are all the things that I did." It's a subtle way of thinking that if we do all these things, we can earn heaven. We think that we can earn those warm-fuzzies. This can come out of our childhood if we were rewarded and affirmed and praised for the things we did. We can transfer some of that to our relationship with God, and it can lead to spiritual avarice. We can even get an attachment in ministry. "Lord, I have to know exactly what You are going to do here. I have to know." That might be what we would like, but that isn't depending upon God. He will let us know what He wants us to know when it's the right time.

This used to bother me a great deal, particularly when I came home from the cloister. I thought I was doing fine in being dependent upon God and trusting Him until a lot of people in the prayer group started asking me questions each Saturday night. "Do you have a place yet?" "No." That didn't bother me. "Well, why not?" "Well, because God hasn't supplied anything yet." "Well, when is He going to do it?" "Well, I don't know." "Well, how are you going to live? Where's the community? When is this all going to start happening?" All these questions!

I would go home to my hermitage every Saturday night from the prayer meeting all discombobulated. My peace was gone, and here I was questioning, "Lord, what about this? What about that?" because everyone else wanted to know. He would calm me down, and by the middle of the week I was just fine again. I don't need to know. In fact, one time He told me, "You don't need to know till I'm ready to let you know. I never am going to tell you the second, third, or fourth steps because you'd only get in My way. Just one step at a time." That's maddening, really! It takes awhile to get used to this dependence upon God because this sin of avarice is in us. We want to know. Maybe you don't have this problem, but it really was grabbing me. Saturday night would come around, and I would be at peace, but then the questions would start again!

We have to be careful because the enemy is lurking so as to rob us of peace and trick us into independence. Have you ever

143

felt like, "Lord, if You don't hurry up and do something, I'm going to do something myself"? We have to be careful not to move out ahead of the Lord.

We have a tendency to exercise ownership, but the early Church held everything in common. So even if we aren't living in a community and holding everything in common, whatever we possess isn't really ours because every good gift, comes from on high. It's all given to us by God. It's all God's gift. It's good for us to remember that the Lord gives and the Lord can take away (see Job 1:21). It's all His.

Avarice will show up in our spiritual lives when we begin to worry about our spiritual failure or inability to pray. We may begin to worry that we're having too many distractions or ugly thoughts or temptations, and we can't get rid of them. In other words, it's all turning in on self. It's not prayer anymore. It isn't taking me to God. Rather it's about me: "I'm not as saintly; I'm not as holy; I'm not as beautiful; I'm not as pleasing to Him as I would like to be." Avarice comes into our prayer because we're afraid to take the risk of relying solely on God and His love for us as we are. We are afraid to rely on God to change us and provide for us. God is the One who is the Benefactor; we are the beneficiary.

Spiritual Warfare

Sin is Satan's territory, so he is very involved in all of these sins. There are a few evil spirits that we run into quite a bit in this particular sin of avarice. There is a spirit called fear of fears where people are afraid of almost everything, and the spirits make sure that you are. There are spirits of deceit and unbelief working because one of the main virtues here is faith. There are spirits called spiritual deceit, fear of rejection, idolatry, larceny, indecision, and nervousness. There is the actual spirit of greed itself.

The part of the armor that we're putting on is the shield of faith. Faith is dominant here. Without that shield of faith, we cannot stop the fiery darts. This is one of the reasons these evil spirits can get to us. They can get past our armor if we're not relying on and using our faith each day. If we're not really believing, those fiery darts then can come right through, and we get on shaky ground.

Remedies

Gift of the Holy Spirit: Understanding

The very special gift of the Holy Spirit that can uproot the sin of avarice is the gift of Understanding. Understanding is a gift of seeing. "Oh, now I see." We can know something, but if we can't understand what God is trying to say to us or show us, it will not bear fruit. Understanding is seeing things more with the eyes of the heart; it's seeing more with faith. We see beneath. We see the mystery. We see the truth. Understanding will open our eyes to the broader picture of what God wants.

We see Jesus using this gift after the Resurrection on the road to Emmaus. Scripture says, "Beginning, then, with Moses and all the prophets, He interpreted for them every passage of Scripture that referred to Him" (Lk 24:27). Wouldn't that be wonderful if He would open our minds to everything in Scripture that pertains to Him? He opened their minds. They could understand it. Only God can do that. This is a gift of Understanding.

We need knowledge in order to open up what we know and to give us the power. We begin to understand the tremendous damage that attachment to anything does to us and what it does to our relationship with God. It's a powerful gift, and it will penetrate these truths. It will penetrate our motives for what we are doing and why we are doing it.

The gift of Understanding penetrates divine truth. It helps us to understand the mystery of Jesus present in the Eucharist in a deeper way. Without the gift of Understanding, we're not going to understand that He is truly there. We know it, and we accept it, but with this gift, we know in a much deeper way that He is really, really present. We know it at such a level that we would give our life that He is present rather than to deny it. We begin to understand the deeper meaning of the Mass and the Sacraments.

Understanding allows us to see through eyes of faith. It's a seeing gift, and we have to see. We're not going to give our lives

145

over to the Father and say, "Into Your hands I commend my spirit" (Lk 23:46), if we don't really see and know this Person who we are putting all of our trust in. We just don't give up our life to the thin air. We have to give it over to Someone we understand.

People who work tirelessly for beautiful causes see the larger vision. They have a motive. They see what the fruit of their labor can be. They have to "see," or they're not going to dedicate their whole lives to any cause. They're driven because they believe in their cause so deeply and can see the good that can come out of it. These beautiful causes get started because people begin to understand, they begin to penetrate a truth and see that it could truly be for God's greater honor and glory or it's going to help other people.

So the gift of Understanding has many aspects. It goes with the Beatitude, "Blessed are the single-hearted for they shall see God" (Mt 5:8). The more we can receive the gift of Understanding and see God, the easier it will be to let go because we have the one Treasure. This generosity of giving and sharing purifies our hearts constantly. The more that we give, the more we will receive and see. Then this gift starts operating in a very deep way.

Our own Archbishop Curtiss has said, "If you don't know the Holy Spirit, you don't know the Church." We need that anointing. We need to be taught by God in a deep rich mystical way, and this gift of Understanding reveals these hidden beauties, these hidden riches. God is so rich and He has so much He wants to share. He wants us to understand so much more, and it's ours for the asking.

This gift of Understanding feeds us. We are so fed when our minds and hearts are illumined by a truth, by a grace. One second before we didn't know, but now we know. We can ponder like Our Lady did. Scripture tells us that Mary kept these things in her heart and pondered them (see Lk 2:51). This is the gift of Understanding. We want to ponder these lights and turn them over like a beautiful diamond, looking at this truth in many different ways. This is contemplation. We may have knowledge of something, but we need this gift to understand the truth that God is sharing with us. We need to see. We need to see God.

Words from the Cross

The seventh word from the Cross is, "Father, into Your hands, I commend my spirit" (Lk 23:46). Into Your hands, I commend my mind, my heart, my memory, my will. Into Your hands, Father, I totally commend my life, which is the ultimate of poverty, the ultimate of detachment. With the seventh word from the Cross, Jesus won this grace for us. The greatest attachment we all have is to ourselves: our own life, our own way of doing things, and our own securities. He is saying, "Let it all go into the Father's hands. Let go of all the control." The gift of Understanding helps us realize that there's more. Whatever we let go of now, God will never be outdone in generosity. Never.

Avarice stands directly opposed to the virtue of charity because charity is going to prompt us to release ownership of anything that we are holding to ourselves. Charity is going to prompt us to give. For those of us in community, the spirit and vow of poverty are very beautiful. Jesus enjoins His disciples to prefer Him to everything and everyone. He bids them to renounce all that they have for His sake and that of the Kingdom. Jesus is asking us to renounce all that we have. St. Paul said, "For your sake, He made Himself poor" (2Cor 8:9). For my sake, for me, He became poor so that I could become rich in His gifts, in His grace, and in His love.

Jesus commended the poor widow who gave all that she had to live on (see Lk 21:4). Jesus gave His all. He did it first. Abraham was willing to give God his only son, Isaac. In order for us to live in the full spirit of poverty, the full spirit of our vow, we really have to look at our "Isaacs." What do we hang on to? What do we have trouble sharing? What would we really get upset over if it was found missing, or someone took it, or even if someone needed it? Is there anything we have that we cannot live without other than Jesus Christ? Jesus calls those who are poor in spirit blessed, happy (Mt 5:3).

We know that there should be a deep joy in not having. There should be happiness in doing without. There should be contentment of heart in not wanting. This would be perfection. So if we need to choose, it's always better to choose less than to choose more. When I was being called out of the cloister, there

147

were several things that I could bring with me. I didn't know what to do so I called my spiritual director. Obviously he knew how to cut through this sin very well because his advice was, "Bring less than more." So I did. I had the clothes on my back, the two-hundred dollars they had given me, and my Bible. And that was it.

Later I thought, "Lord, I hope we really heard You. I'm out here on the waters right now." About the second day, we were driving along the highway and some men were putting up a big billboard. They were rolling out the very top of the sign as our car went zooming by. It said, "We're with you." I never forgot that! It steadied me right away—He was with me. I had known that He was with me in the cloister, but now I needed to know that He was with me now. I knew the Trinity was with me. We need confirmation from time to time, especially whenever we are trying to detach from something. We need to ask for confirmations because they will help steady us. The Holy Spirit steadies us. He is the Confirmer. He loves to confirm us and affirm us as well.

Our thoughts then should be not on how much the vow of poverty imposes on us but on what we can do to carry out the vow more fully. If we practice the spirit of the vow of poverty in little ways, like shunning anything that would be giving into the tendency toward avarice in thought, word, and deed, then we will be uprooting this sin from the enclosed garden within.

The spirit of poverty will be safeguarded if the will of our superiors or those who are responsible for us is accepted fully and joyfully. God loves a cheerful giver (2Cor 9:7). So in this spirit of poverty, which comes against this vice of avarice, we are always ready to accede to the superior, to surrender to God's will coming through the authorities in our lives. We are ready to let our conscience, and the conscience and will of our superior, in a sense, be our guides. This is one of the beauties of having a Holy Father who is head of the Church because father knows best. We are set free to give our wills over to what he is teaching in the name of Jesus and in the name of the Church. This sets us free to be busy about our Father's business.

I think the beauty of coming against avarice is that it brings us into a deep relationship with the Father, that He is our Provider. It brings us into a beautiful experience of Divine Providence. The fruits that come forth during and after the struggle are tremendous joy and freedom and a deep love that will want to live and not count the cost. We are free! We may be poor, but we're free. We are especially free of ourselves, which is the greatest attachment of all. We are free from worry and concern. A true poverty of spirit will come forth, a very deep trust and belief that God is my Father and He will take care of me in all things. We are not alone. We are in this together. We will be totally content and at peace to have Him as our sole (soul) support. This is the grace that Jesus won for us on the Cross.

It is the spirit of poverty that enables us to give and sets us totally free from this sin of avarice. We all are called to live the spirit of poverty, renunciation, and interior detachment more deeply. The vow and promise of poverty do not of itself do away with the tendency to attach to earthly goods, but it does seek to regulate it through exterior and interior renunciation. We need to keep the spirit of the law regarding the vow and promise of poverty, not just the letter of the law. It is the spirit of the vows and promises that really protect and safeguard them.

Our Lady lived out of a true poverty of spirit. She was the poorest of the poor and the richest of the rich. She had it all because she was so detached. She was so empty of self, so she could be totally filled with God. She was full of grace, meaning God's life, full of love. She wants us to be filled as she was. She wants us to be full of God, and that's what we want. But there is that little step that has to be taken, almost daily sometimes, to make room for God and to make room for His gifts. This true poverty of spirit is something we need to ask for. Then when God starts to show us things daily, we can remember that we just asked for the gift and let them go. We need to let them go. He will never be outdone in generosity, I assure you, never. He always gives a hundredfold, always much more than we can even ask or imagine.

Virtues:
Generosity, Faith

It takes tremendous generosity to give our all: to give our life, our heart, our soul, and our spirit. This is how Jesus put this sin to death. Generosity will help counteract avarice because the more we give, the more detached we will become. So detachment and purity of heart are extremely important. In other words, we want to keep in check even the desire and love of things. It is focusing more on giving than receiving. Interestingly, the more we give, the more we receive. In the book of Sirach we read, "Give to the Most High as he has given to you, generously, according to your means. For the Lord is one who always repays, and he will give back to you sevenfold" (Sir 35:9-10). Giving away ourselves and what we receive in prayer is going to detach us from the desire of ownership. He's given us beautiful words to keep this particular sin from possessing us. He gives us these gifts to balance us so we're not out of control or in bondage to any of these sins. Generosity, coming out of charity, is probably one of the most powerful virtues there is to come against avarice. We can beg for the virtue of generosity to really give all that we have, all that we are, our best selves, each day to the Lord.

One time when we were in Medjugorje praying, instead of enjoying the things at Medjugorje, Our Lady was bringing the problems in the United States to us. So we found ourselves in constant intercession for America when we were in Medjugorje. One of the things she showed us was an image of a big city. Our Lady was like a bag lady picking up this and picking up that. She was letting us understand that she will take anything we have to give her. She wants anything we have. If we can only give her something that's left over, she'll take it. She wants us to learn to give. She won't refuse anything we have. Whatever we have, she'll take it. Then she kind of cleans it up, purifies it, and gives it to God.

So if we don't have all of ourselves to give to God every day, we can give what we have. If we just have a tiny bit, we can give it to Our Lady, and she can magnify it somehow and make it very acceptable to the Father. This will get us into the habit of trying to be generous, to give and give and share with others what they need. It might be a prayer. It might be a smile. It might be a helping hand. It might be some kind of affirmation. If we are more sensitive to the movement of the Spirit within, He will show us what it is that He would like us to give. He is a giver because He's a lover. We can become a lover and learn to give away what we have received, particularly the spiritual gifts.

It is good to meditate on the poverty of Jesus and on His freedom and His total detachment. He led a life of detachment, which prepared Him for His final full detachment on the Cross, "Father, into Your hands I commend my spirit"(Lk 23:46). That came from a lifetime of detachment. In our daily life, we can embrace detachment, even if only in a small way, by using only what is necessary, not everything I desire.

This deep spirit of poverty enables us to give, and the giving itself fosters and feeds the spirit of poverty. This means that we take care of the things that God has given to us. However God has provided for us, we learn to take care of what He has given to us, and we have a healthy care and concern for these things.

Faith is one of the main virtues to counteract greed. If we really believe that God loves us and we are His child and He is our Provider, then this whole aspect of giving, letting go, and not hanging onto everything becomes easier. Sharing and not wanting to possess becomes easier because we want to be totally His and have nothing other than Him. We really have to believe He's going to be there for us. We really have to believe Jesus when He says, "I am with you always" (Mt 28:20). We really have to believe that. Faith is a tremendous virtue that helps us to really believe with our whole heart and soul that God will provide whatever we need.

So the fruit here is a very deep trust and belief that God will take care of me in all things. We're content to have Him do that. We can rest in knowing that God will take care of us just like children are totally content that they are going to be fed, carried, and taken care of. In the spiritual life we allow God to carry us; we're not trying to carry ourselves.

One time I was meditating on Jesus calling Peter out of the boat to walk on the waters. I could really relate with that because in the cloister I was quite safe, content, and secure, never ever thinking I would be called out. So when He called Peter out of the boat and onto the waters, this passage really came near and dear to my heart. For a long time I meditated on Peter and his courage and fortitude and the love he had for Jesus to walk on water until I began to realize, "Oh my goodness, this isn't natural." As I started getting used to walking on the waters of leaving the cloister and was very sure now of the Lord being there, my focus shifted in prayer one day—Jesus also was on the water—and so my question that day was, "Lord, what kept You up? You were on the waters, too." He said, "My Father's love. My Father's love always held Me." We all need to know that. The Father holds us - the Father's love. It's His love that always holds us. So we don't need to hold on to anything. We can totally let go and this sin won't have a hold on us.

Mary Magdalene used to spend a great deal of time at Jesus' feet. She was being fed. She really got to know Jesus and the heart of Jesus. When Jesus called her by name after the Resurrection, she recognized His voice. She said, "Rabbouni" (Jn 20:16) and started to cling to Him. Wouldn't you if you thought someone you loved so desperately was dead and now they're alive? I mean, she was hanging on for dear life! And what does He say to her? "Do not cling to Me, Mary" (see Jn 20:17). "Let go. Let go and really become little." A little baby doesn't cling. A little baby doesn't hold onto anything. A baby is totally held. That's the full conversion process that God is calling us to—to be so little that we can't hang on. We can only allow ourselves to be held, totally trusting the One who is holding us. This gift of faith is how we can put this sin to death.

Additional Helps

To help us come against this sin of avarice, we can begin and end each day with prayer. We can keep our eyes focused on God. We can generously give all that we have to God. We can embrace the First Commandment to love the Lord, our God, with our *whole* heart, our *whole* mind, and our *whole* strength. It's not easy to keep that commandment.

Sometimes we think we have to know everything that God knows, or we always want to know more than He wants us to know. That's avarice. A way to come against this is to choose to want to know only what God thinks is necessary for us to know. Sometimes He deliberately doesn't let us know, and that's fine, but then we have to look at, "Why do I have to know? What's in me that I need to know?" I realized I didn't really need to know. I came out of the cloister at peace with all the things I didn't know, but when people started to constantly ask questions, I found out that I wanted to please them. I wanted to answer them. Finally I thought, "They don't need to know either." So no one knew.

We can resist avarice by joyfully living a life in love with God. We can work toward our interior perfection by pleasing God, not ourselves or others. It doesn't mean that my daily activities are going to change or be different, but my motive can definitely change. Instead of hurrying up to get something over with, we can slow down and be aware that we are doing this for the Lord. It makes such a difference. It will give us wings. We will start to feel joyous and light because whatever we are doing is not being done in vain. We are doing it for God, and He sees everything and will give us our just reward Himself.

We can trust that God will do all that is necessary to purify us, to take care of us, and to answer our prayers. We don't have to think of a lot of penance that we can do. Again, we have to fight that independence within us that we should do this or we need to do that, which is more the adult way. The way of avarice tells us to be more independent, even in the things we're doing for the Lord. We *can* wait for the light of the Holy Spirit. At Fatima, Our Lady said that we need to learn to accept what God puts into our lives each day. In other words, we need to learn to accept the people in our life today, to accept the conversations today, and to accept the way things go today. This can be a tremendous penance and purification.

We can try to use only what is really necessary (not the surplus, not everything we desire) and use what God has given us with great respect. We are trying to come against those desires that are not of God and root them out. We can share and tithe. Maybe only some can tithe with money, but we all can tithe with our time and the gifts and talents that God has given to us. We can all tithe with whatever we hold dear, and we can share it with someone else. There's always some way to give. If nothing else, there is always prayer.

We want to watch any desires to control or maintain ownership. In the early church community, they held everything in common (see Acts 3:44). They had this state of mind and this deep spirit of poverty. They were coming against avarice perfectly because they had no ownership. For those of us under vows of poverty that means that we take care of everything as though it belongs to me personally, in the sense that I am responsible. I'm responsible for the way that I take care of my missal, the way I care for my office books, the way I take care of the cars, the way I take care of the clothes I wear because everything is in common, and it (whatever "it" is) belongs to more than just me. It belongs to the Lord and it is on loan to all of us.

153

Begin this examination of conscience
by placing yourself in the Lord's presence.
Become aware of His love surrounding you
and filling you to overflowing.
Be filled with the desire to draw into closer union
with the Father, Son, and Holy Spirit.
Choose to let go of anything that is
preventing you from this union.

EXAMINATION OF CONSCIENCE—AVARICE

Daily Life

Do I have an inordinate love and desire to possess and hoard things? money? knowledge? time? talent?

In what areas of my life have I become overly materialistic?
  Has this materialism and desire to possess caused harm to myself, my family, or community?
  What things do I desire which I cannot have?

Do I look to my possessions and bank account for security?
  Do I feel fearful when my self-sufficiency is threatened?

St. Paul said, "The love of money is the root of all evil" (1Tm 6:10). Do I believe this?
  Do I have an inordinate need to possess?
  Has my excessive desire to possess and accumulate riches ever led me to lying, fraud, restlessness, hard-heartedness, or violence?

Where is my selfishness and self-centeredness robbing my family and community of resources?
  How does my excessive desire to accumulate affect my willingness to share with those less fortunate than myself?
  In what ways do I display a true spirit of generosity?
  In what ways do I need to be more generous?

Where do I see that my love for money is leading me away from the Lord?

Do I have a false attachment to home, amusements, books, furniture, or precious things?

First Commandment: "I am the Lord your God; you shall not have strange gods before me."

On what occasions do I adore and make money and earthly possessions my god?

Do I experience a normal, healthy use of things as a *means* to live a comfortable life, or have these things become the *ends*?

In what cases do I "worship" the created good rather than the Creator?

Do I experience more satisfaction in possessing things than in the things themselves?

Do I run the risk of having my passion to possess things take over and possess me instead?

On what occasions do I sacrifice everything (my family, time, and energies) in order to possess and accumulate additional wealth?

What can I do in order to get a proper balance between providing for my family and trusting in the Lord to provide?

Do I hoard because I do not trust that God will provide?

Will I do anything necessary to possess riches?

Tenth Commandment: "You shall not covet your neighbor's goods."

Do I desire to amass worldly goods without limit?

Do I feel more powerful as my net worth increases?

Do I always want more than I need?

What are the areas of attachment where I still do not let the Father have control?

How does seeing what others have that I don't have but want, hinder me from living simply?

In my spiritual life

How grateful am I?

Is the Lord my only wealth?

Do I cling to my good works in an effort to earn heaven?

In what ways do I seek first God's kingship and His way of holiness?

What is preventing me from embracing the Cross with both hands?

In what ways do I run from mortification and spiritual poverty?

When do I have difficulty saying, "Into Your hands I commend my spirit"?

Am I truly generous in giving my life to the Lord?

In what areas am I greedy with my life?

Where do I need to embrace this charism of intercession more wholeheartedly?

Do I generously allow this battle for souls to rage within myself and my family?

In what ways have I experienced, "Yet I live, no longer I, but Christ lives in me" (Gal 2:20).

Where do I need to depend more on God and less on things?

Where is this dependence on God most frightening and difficult for me?

Where do I have difficulty keeping my eyes focused on Jesus?

Am I willing to let go of all my good actions and works?

Have I become so attached to spiritual consolations that I become unhappy when no longer receiving them?

Am I attached to religious practices, devotions, rituals, sacramentals, and religious articles?

Vow / Promise of Poverty

Is my vow / promise of poverty a cause for joy in my life?

Where do I experience joy in my vow / promise of poverty?

What am I doing to embrace this vow / promise more fully?

What can I do to become more detached interiorly?

Where is my poverty a "burden"?

Where is this not a whole-hearted gift?

In what ways do I break this vow / promise of poverty?

Do I keep the spirit or the letter of the law regarding poverty?

Where do I experience joy in doing without?

Where has the Lord been pointing out that I need to be more detached from material goods?

Do I allow my affections to be unduly strong for persons, places, or things?

Community / Family Life

How do I show my respect for the things that are intended for common use?

Do I take more than what is my fair share?

Do I have a sense of ownership of communal property?

Am I possessive of my things?

In what ways do I readily share my goods, time, love, and talent?

156

Do my actions or lack of action cause another to fall into the sin of avarice?

Consider one or two areas where you struggle with avarice the most. Does there seem to be a common thread or reason why you struggle in these areas? Journal any insights and feelings with the Lord. Listen for His words of love and counsel. Throughout the week take time to ponder, "What profit would there be for one to gain the whole world and forfeit his life?" (Mt 16:26) Journal.

Conclusion

The root of each of the Capital Sins is fear, which is rooted into Satan, the deceiver himself. The remedy is love. This is why we keep going back to the Cross and nailing our sin to the Cross because love is the root of all healing and deliverance. It is that simple. The Cross is central. It is the summit of everything. It is total freedom. "Perfect love casts out all fear" (1Jn 4:18). Love can sever each of the Capital Sins and their ramifications because it is perfect love. With this agape love, the power of this love, we can nail all of our sins to the Cross.

Through repentance and the Sacrament of Reconciliation, we are defeating Satan by the Blood of the Lamb and the word of our testimony (Rv 12:11) because we are allowing all of these sins and their roots to be totally washed away and removed.

Anger

The root of anger is basically a fear of forgiving. Ultimately, we're going to get to the fear that if I forgive, I'm going to be hurt again. Anger is rooted in the fear of forgiving and the fear of rejection. We are afraid to let our protection (our anger) go because it will leave us very vulnerable to be hurt again. Piety is the gift of loving the Father and loving His people with our whole heart and our whole soul and our neighbor as ourselves, and it will give us that strength, that grace to forgive and to uproot this fear. "Father forgive them."

Envy

Envy is rooted into a fear of being powerless. It's a fear of giving up control. It's a fear of getting out of the driver's seat. It's a fear of totally letting go. It's a fear of that total surrender. This is why the gift of Wisdom is so key because the highest form of wisdom is surrender. It takes agape power. It takes that kind of love to let go. Jesus went on the Cross primarily because

158

of His tremendous love of the Father. He did it for the Father so that we could be with Him through all eternity. This gift of Wisdom will give us the same motive: to lay down our lives for the Father and others as well. Wisdom will totally uproot this fear of giving up control. It will allow us to surrender and enjoy each day, Paradise with Jesus. "This day you will be with me in paradise."

Lust

Lust is rooted in the fear of being a child. It's a fear of being little because in being little we go through the conversion process and become pure like a child. This is why this third word of the Cross is so key, "Behold your Mother." If we're not a little child, we don't really need a mother. Children need a mother. When we are close to Mary and are consecrated to her, she will get us those graces to be pure of heart, to be little. She knows how to mother. At her appearance as Our Lady of Guadalupe, Mary said to Juan Diego, "Have I not placed you in my heart and made you my responsibility?" Yes, we live in the heart of Mary. We are her responsibility. She will keep us pure. The great gift of Fear of the Lord will give us a tremendous dislike to do anything that will displease God or Our Lady as well.

Pride

Pride is rooted into fear of submitting my will to another, whether it is human authority or Divine authority. It's a fear of depending upon someone else who knows. Pride is rooted in a fear of submitting my will to God's will because I'm going to go into that fearful atmosphere of "whatever," and I don't know. It is a fear of the unknown if I give God my will. The beautiful gift of Counsel will help us learn to ask and ask. We know that God will help us. In so many Scriptures, Jesus says, "Ask. Ask." Jesus knew we had to take Counsel, or we wouldn't know truth. We wouldn't be able to come into freedom and maintain that freedom, so we ask. We even ask like He did at times. Particularly when we're in heavy intercession, we'll cry out,

"My God, my God. Why have You abandoned me? Why have You left me hanging here in this deep intercession?" He will often say, "Just hang on a little while longer. I'm using you because we're coming against pride right now. I'm setting some people free right now, and I'm getting Satan out of their lives." We never know what He's going to say or do.

Gluttony

Gluttony is the fear of mortification, fear of the Cross, and fear of decreasing. It's a fear of putting my false self to death (not my true self, not my best self). We definitely need the gift of Fortitude to fight this sin because it's a tremendous struggle. We saw Jesus struggling with the Father's will in this regard in the Garden. It's a costly struggle to put something to death. It might be so tiny that no one even knows about it, but it can be costly. We do this so that we can enter into God's thirst for souls, His thirst for love, which means everything to God so that His redemption was not in vain. "I thirst."

Sloth

Sloth is rooted in fear of commitment. As long as I can stay busy, busy, busy then I don't have to be committed because I'm too busy. The root of sloth is fear of being committed to God and prayer, which connects us to God. Sloth doesn't want to commit to anything, to anyone, or to any project. It has that lazy dimension. It doesn't want to commit to the spiritual life. We need this gift of Knowledge to see things from God's point of view. We need the grace to finish the work God has given us to do, whatever our vocation is. We need the grace to finish what God has given us to do on a day-to-day basis. Often we get frustrated because we might not have achieved our goal for the day. But maybe we did finish what God had given us to do. We only know that if we are in prayer with Him daily. Daily prayer is key in all of this. Jesus taught us to pray that way, "Father, give us *today* our daily bread." Not the bread for tomorrow, but what I need to feed me today so that I in turn can nurture others and give it away as You see fit. "It is finished."

Avarice

Avarice is rooted in the fear of detachment, the fear of giving all, the fear of letting go. It's a fear of total dependence on God and letting go of my own independence because I think my own independence is freedom (which it really isn't). It's a fear of totally giving over one's life into the hands of the Father. But once the gift of Understanding is operative within us, and we really understand who the Father is, then we will want to give ourselves totally into His hands. "Father, into your hands I commend my spirit."

Each of the Capital Sins has one common root—fear. Each of the gifts of the Holy Spirit has one common root—love. God is telling us that through His beautiful gifts His perfect love will cast out fear and uproot our sin so that we will know that freedom and joy that only truth can bring about within us.

There's a story that a priest told us when he was at a parade at Mardi Gras in New Orleans. The floats were coming loaded with all these toys and trinkets that were being tossed to the crowd right and left. The children were lined up along the street. He said he was watching this little boy who was right in front of him catch these little trinkets and souvenirs. He had both hands filled with this stuff, hanging on for dear life.

Now half a block away, this priest could see another float coming with beautiful stuffed animals on it. He said, "I wonder what he's going to do when he sees that float." This little boy was so rich, holding his treasures really close to himself so he wouldn't drop anything. As the float got closer, Father said you could see the indecision. "What am I going to do? Oh, I want that, but look I have all this." The float was right in front of him now, and he made the decision to let everything go and caught a big stuffed animal as it came.

This is what we're talking about—when we can let go of everything so that we can really go for the gold, get the real Treasure. Then we have put this sin to death as well. Then we can say also, "Father, into Your hands I can give my spirit now because it's free. It's not clinging to anything. I've let all of those attachments go. I'm free to come totally to You now and Your way."

Jesus was speaking to His Apostles at the Last Supper and said, "I have greatly desired to eat this Passover with you" (Lk 22:15). He has greatly desired to share this meal with us. He wants to share the Passover with us. He knows the struggle. He wants to share our journey from death into life, out of darkness into light, out of bondage into freedom, and out of fear into love.

But Satan doesn't want us to make that passover. In Revelation 12, we see the dragon takes its place by the sea, right where the land and water touch. He's right there at that dividing line trying to prevent us from making the passover from what is earthy into what is spiritual. There is a dying process that goes on, but there is a living process. There's a decreasing, as John the Baptist tells us, and an increasing of the life of the Lord within us. It will cost us our lives. We have to die to make the passover.

We are people making the passover out of death into life so that we can help the Church to make that passover. God doesn't want us to do it alone. It entails the Cross and sacrifice. There is sacrifice that is necessary to come against each of these sins. There's mortification. There's a dying. But Jesus said, "I have greatly desired to eat this Passover with you" (Lk 22:15). In other words, "Don't leave Me out. While you are denying yourself these different things, I will be feeding you with Life because I don't want you to die."

Replacing our fear with His perfect love

Fear can control us in so many ways. So if you find the emotion of fear rising, then follow it through. Ask the Lord, "Where did this begin?" Even more importantly, "Lord, replace this fear with Your perfect love."

I remember when the Lord asked me to consecrate myself to the Holy Spirit. I hadn't really thought about that. I'm so used to the consecration to the Heart of Jesus and the consecration to Our Lady. One day, it was to consecrate myself to the Holy Spirit. Immediately, I had an emotion of fear. I was in touch with it instantly, and it surprised me. I thought, "What in the world? Why would I be afraid of the Holy Spirit?" I thought I was living very much in the Holy Spirit, and now at the thought of consecrating myself totally to the Holy Spirit I could feel this emotion of fear rising. The heart will tell us things that the mind won't. The mind has to be very logical and have it all together. But here my heart was stirring up this fear.

So I asked God about it right away. "Where did this come from? Why am I afraid of this consecration?" The Lord let me understand, "Because in your heart you know how generous the Holy Spirit is. You know that He gives everything away and that if you consecrate yourself to Him, He's going to give you away, too." That's exactly right. That was truth. That was the fear: that I didn't belong to myself anymore. There is still a little bit of myself wanting a little bit of control of my life. "I've given God almost everything, but I'm going to hang onto some little part of it here."

So it's best to let the heart have its way because that's what God wants. He said, "Blessed are the poor in spirit (blessed are we if we're being given away and if we give ourselves totally to God) because the reign of God is theirs" (Mt 5:3). We get the whole Kingdom and the beautiful fruits of the Kingdom here on earth. Here and now we can have that Kingdom alive within us.

We want to be attached to Jesus Christ Crucified, to Jesus on the Cross, because this is agape love. It's pure love. It's perfect love. Perfect love has the power of deliverance to set the captives free because it casts out all fear. Perfect love casts out all fear. It's also the power of evangelization. Jesus said, "And I, once I am lifted up from the earth, will draw all men to myself" (Jn 12:32). So if we're after conversions and graces for people, we need to stay with Jesus on the Cross because we have a power then. Our prayers will have a tremendous power. Look at what happened with those who stood by Jesus on the Cross. There weren't many, but their whole lives were so special. We see the fruit of Jesus being lifted up at Pentecost. When we allow God to lift us up and nail us there with Himself on the Cross, we will see fruit in our intercession like we've never seen before. We will see many mini-Pentecosts happening in people's lives because we are releasing this tremendous love power to others through the pierced heart of Jesus.

Jesus said, "There is no greater love than this: to lay down one's life for one's friends" (Jn 15:13). We lay down our life.

163

We lay down the sin. We lay down all these imperfections that we want to go. We lay down our wills. We lay down our opinions. We lay them down for our Friend, Jesus. As we lay down our lives, we receive more life. It's a win-win situation. We can't lose.

God said, "Precious in the eyes of the Lord is the death His faithful ones" (Ps 116:15). God sees us as very precious in His sight when we can lay down our lives and take up the life of His Son instead, when we can let go of our false selves and begin to live out of our true identities as His children. This is who we truly are. We were meant to be free. God's truth and love have set us free. He's given us the power and the wisdom in turn to help others become free as well.

This becomes a lifestyle for us. It's the lifestyle for prayer warriors. Peter said, "Consecrated by the Spirit to a life of obedience to Jesus Christ and purification with His Blood" (1Pt 1:2). That's our lifestyle: to be consecrated by the Spirit to a life of obedience. "Yes, Lord. Be it done unto me according to Your Word." In this consecration to Jesus Christ and purification with His Blood, we are constantly taking our sins to the Cross. As we become burden-bearers, we take the sins of others as well as our own sins to the Cross so that God may be fully honored and worshipped and glorified in all things, as is His due. I am telling you all of this today so that His "joy may be in each one of you and your joy may be complete" (Jn 15:11).

"Rouse the Warriors to Arms"

Joel, the great prophet, said, "Declare this among the nations: Proclaim a war. Rouse the warriors to arms! Let all your soldiers report and march! Beat your plowshares into swords" (Jl 4:9-10). Plowshares prepare the soil. This is what intercession does: it prepares hearts to receive God's Word. But now He is saying to us, "Take your intercessory gifts and be changed into swords. You are going to go forth into battle now." The times are different. The signs of the times are very clear. The handwriting is on the wall that we are being prepared for battle. So our intercessory tools are going to change and develop more into prayer-warrior tools. It means that we need to allow the Spirit to change us into that sword with Jesus because Jesus is the Sword of the Spirit. As we come into this deeper covenant union with Jesus, we become the weapon the Spirit is looking for so that He can come forth with this warfare.

Recently we had a beautiful Spirit-led Rosary at Bellwether. In imagery, the room where we were praying began filling with angels. Then the Holy Spirit came. He was huge, wingtip to wingtip, taking up the entire room. Obviously He had our attention! He was the focus. Surrounding Him were angels with trumpets. Then there was this incredible silence. Silence fell upon the whole room. We were aware of the silence and His presence.

The angels were circling the room, and with their trumpets they were announcing something, but we didn't understand. So we asked, "What is it that You want us to know?" We could focus in on the Holy Spirit a little more closely and saw a small scroll within His beak. It had a little golden handle that we could pull down to read the scroll. We asked Him, "What is on the scroll?"

He took us to Revelation 8:1. "When the Lamb broke open the seventh seal, there was silence in heaven for about half an hour." When God is going to move in a sovereign way, there is always silence. Have you noticed that? The silence of the Annunciation, the silence of Bethlehem, the silence of Nazareth, and the silence of the Resurrection. Ponder the silence of the Eucharist. When God is truly present, He speaks through the silence. He gets our attention in the silence.

Next He took us to Revelation 8:2. "Then as I watched, the seven angels who minister in God's presence were given seven trumpets." There they were. Then He took us to Revelation 10: 1-7. "Then I saw another mighty angel come down from heaven wrapped in a cloud." (Often a cloud is symbolic of God's presence—the cloud of unknowing, the cloud that surrounded Moses as He made his trek across the desert.) So here is this mighty angel, wrapped in a cloud, wrapped in God's presence, with a rainbow about his head. Immediately that spoke to us of covenant love and union. "And in his hand, he held a little scroll which had been opened. Then he raised his right hand to heaven and he took an oath, 'There shall be no more delay.' When the time comes for the seventh angel to blow his trumpet, the mysterious plan of God which he announced to his servants, the prophets, shall be accomplished in full." We knew that God was trying to announce something to us about His mysterious plan and that it was going to be accomplished in full. There would be no more delay. It was time.

Revelation 10:9 went on to inform us, "I went up to the angel and said to him, 'Give me the little scroll.' He said to me, 'Here, take and eat it. It will be sour in your stomach, but in your mouth, it will taste sweet as honey'." We thought, "That's just like Jesus. When He calls us, when He asks anything of us, there's nothing sweeter. There's absolutely nothing sweeter than to hear from Jesus Christ and to have that Word come alive within us, but sometimes He is saying or asking of us is hard to digest.

What He is asking of us as prayer warriors is very sweet, but yet it's very difficult to be a prayer warrior. It is a very difficult ministry. Even though we know God is with us, there are times when it is hard to digest. There are times when we might be tempted to say, "Lord, choose someone else. Help! I just want to sit under this tree and rest." But this is the mysterious plan.

Everything about God is mystery. We'll never know Him fully here, and yet He says, "Come up here and I will show you what must take place in time to come" (Rv 4:2). God was beginning to reveal to us His mysterious plan, this new covenant that He wants to establish now, this New Jerusalem, His glorified Church, people fully alive and filled with the presence of God.

So we began asking the obvious question: "How is this going to be done?" He brought back to mind a word He had given me a year before. He had said, "Prepare My Second Coming." So I wrote down, "Prepare for My Second Coming." He said, "No, that's *not* what I said. I said, 'Prepare My Second Coming.' " At the time, I didn't realize that there was a difference, but there is a difference. When we prepare something, we actually bring it into visibility.

My mind started going. "Let me have an illustration of preparing something, Lord." He said, "When you are preparing dinner, you're not preparing for someone to come. You're preparing the meal. You are bringing it into visibility. It happens." I began to pick up His thinking a little bit. "Then when we are to prepare Your Second Coming, we are going to make it visible?" He said, "Yes." That was quite a revelation to me because I have heard things about the Second Coming. We have received things in prayer, and it has always been focused on different ways of Jesus coming. It never dawned on me that He would be calling prayer warriors into preparing His Second Coming. I never knew that He means that He's coming as the Prayer Warrior Himself. He's coming as the Warrior King. He's coming for the final confrontation with Satan.

He Himself is preparing the place, the dwelling place, in, with, and through us, for this new covenant relationship, this deep union, this Glorified Church where He's fully alive. This was a shock and a reversal of our thinking. We asked for confirmation, and it came again through the Book of Revelation. "He wore a cloak that had been dipped in blood and his name was the Word of God. The armies of heaven were behind him riding white horses (that means they were empowered, that's pure God-power) and dressed in fine linen, pure and white" (Rv 19:13). To be dressed in fine linen pure and white means to be dressed once again in our baptismal robes.

Pope Paul VI wrote about this to the whole Church in his encyclical *Evangelization in the Modern World*. He said that we need to be re-baptized and cleansed of all sin. We need to be totally free of the enemy's camp, which is sin. We are these people riding with Jesus in power, in baptismal robes, washed in the Blood of the Lamb. Hopefully through this study on the

Capital Sins, we have been able to really wash our robes clean. Scripture says, "They defeated him (Satan) by the Blood of the Lamb and by the Word of their testimony" (Rv 12:11). We need to have our baptismal robes on again if we want to win. We have to be clothed with the same cloak dipped in the Blood of the Lamb.

Scripture tells us, "Out of His mouth came a sharp sword" (Rv 19:15). Through the power of the Spirit, the Word of God, now enfleshed within us, is trying to change us day by day by day into Jesus, that Sword. So this mysterious plan is simply that He's coming as warrior, with, in, and through us to prepare a dwelling place of Trinitarian love within each soul. The time is now. Won't this be a beautiful Church when the Trinity is fully alive again within every person? Oh, it's a wonderful dream! It's God's dream, so we know it's going to come true.

The Lord said, "I, the Lord, have called you for the victory of justice. I have grasped you by the hand; I formed you, and set you as a covenant of the people, a light for the nations, to open the eyes of the blind" (Is 42:6-7). We are called to open the eyes of the blind and come against this deception. We are called "to bring out prisoners from confinement, and from the dungeon, those who live in darkness" (Is 42:7). Darkness usually means sin. If we're going to get graces for people to get out of sin, we're going to have to fight for them because we're going right into Satan's camp to get them. That's where he lives. We're going to be a Church on the offensive, literally going into the places where Satan dwells and is holding people in bondage in order to set the captives free.

There's a beautiful prophetic word in Romans 9:17 that I believe is for us. It says, "This is why I raised you up: that through you I might show my power, and my name might be proclaimed throughout all the earth." In other words—this is why I have raised you up. This is why I have called you. This is why I have grasped you by the hand, so that through you I might show My power (it's God's power, not our power) so that My name will be proclaimed throughout all the earth.

As we become more aware of God's power, as we decrease so that He increases, hopefully our whole life will become a Magnificat. God who is mighty has already done great things for us. I know many of you are seasoned intercessors. Many of you have been through many battles, and so you know that the cost is high. It cost Jesus His life, and it will cost us ours as well. But we

168

receive so much more. When we lay down our lives, He gives us more than we could ever imagine. He will never be outdone in generosity.

Exposing the enemy's territory within ourselves has helped us to become freer, so we are in those baptismal robes. More of the evil one's strategies have been exposed. We have learned from God how He wants us to attack and how He wants us to go forth in power and in love, truth, and light.

The Lord was recently teaching me about Sarah when she was informed that she was going to become pregnant, she laughed. So the Lord asked Abraham, "Why did Sarah laugh?" Sarah told Him, "Oh I didn't laugh." Scripture went on to say, "She lied because she was afraid" (see Gn 18:15). That was very anointed for me, and so later in my prayer time, I asked the Lord why that was that so anointed. "Why did she lie out of fear?" He brought to my mind that Satan is a liar. I asked Jesus, "Then does Satan lie also because he's afraid?" Jesus said, "Yes." I said, "Why? What is He afraid of?" The Lord said, "He's afraid of truth because truth sets you free, and Satan does not want you to be set free." He wants us to live out of lies and to stay in the lie. So I took it one more question, "But Lord, You are Truth." I could almost feel Him smiling like, "You're beginning to get it." I said, "Well then, since You are Truth, then Satan is afraid of You." He said, "That's right." I thought, "There's nothing to worry about. Imagine Satan's biggest fear is Jesus." I can't imagine anyone being afraid of Jesus, particularly a prayer warrior.

Jesus is the One we hang onto. Jesus is our best friend. The Father has called us to come into union with His Son, and when we do, we have been empowered in a special way with the Holy Spirit. We live and move and have our whole being in the atmosphere of God. We can go forth with such confidence that Satan is afraid of us, instead of the other way around.

The one little problem is that Satan somehow knows that many of us don't know that God is really within and so we have this power. So we go back to Mount Sinai and listen to God tell Moses (and us), "I will be with you. I will be with you" (Ex 3:12). If we don't really believe that, then we need to take it to prayer. Once upon a time, I didn't believe that all the time. I didn't believe it morning, noon, and night. I didn't believe it when the sun wasn't shining or when things weren't going very well. I began to see that my faith wasn't that strong. When we find ourselves weak in faith, all we have to do is ask the Father for the gift of faith. We need it so we can believe all the time that He is with us always. Then we have a stronghold. Then we're going to stand firm and nothing is going to shake us. Those fiery darts cannot penetrate our shield because we know that we know that we know that God is with us always.

I now understand why John said, "For there is one greater in you than there is in the world" (1Jn 4:4). I now understand why the One within us is greater than all the legions of fallen angels in the world. He is greater than anything in the world. He is God Himself.